PRESIDENT'S MALARIA INITIATIVE

Madagascar

Malaria Operational Plan FY 2016

TABLE OF CONTENTS

ABBREVIATIONS and ACRONYMS

ACT	Artemisinin-based combination therapy
AMM	*Agence du Médicament de Madagascar*
ANC	Antenatal care
AS/AQ	Artesunate-amodiaquine
BCC	Behavior change communication
CCDS	*Comité Communal du Développement Sanitaire*/ Community Health Development Committee
CDC	Centers for Disease Control and Prevention
CHL	Central Highlands
CHV	Community Health Volunteer
CSB	*Centre de Santé de Base*/ Basic Heath Center
DHS	Demographic and Health Survey
DLP	*Direction de la Lutte contre le Paludisme*/ Malaria Control Branch
EPI	Expanded Program on Immunization
FBO	Faith-based Organization
FY	Fiscal year
GHI	Global Health Initiative
Global Fund	Global Fund to Fight AIDS, Tuberculosis and Malaria
GoM	Government of Madagascar
HF	Health Facility
HMIS	Health Management Information System
HSS	Health Systems Strengthening
HW	Health Worker
iCCM	Integrated Community Case Management
IDSR	Integrated Disease Surveillance and Response
IEC	Information, education, communication
IPM	*Institut Pasteur de Madagascar*
IPTp	Intermittent preventive treatment for pregnant women
IRS	Indoor residual spraying
ITN	Insecticide-treated mosquito net
KAP	Knowledge, attitude, practices
LLIN	Long-lasting insecticide-treated net
MDG	Millennium Development Goal
M&E	Monitoring and evaluation
MIP	Malaria in pregnancy
MIS	Malaria Indicator Survey
MoH	Ministry of Health
MOP	Malaria Operational Plan
NMCP	National Malaria Control Program
NGO	Non-governmental Organization
NSP	National Strategic Plan for malaria
OP	Organophosphate
PCV	Peace Corps Volunteer
PhaGDis	*Pharmacie de Gros de District*/ District Pharmaceutical Depot
PMI	President's Malaria Initiative

RA	Resident Advisor
RBM	Roll Back Malaria
RDT	Rapid diagnostic test
SALAMA	Madagascar Central Medical Store
SP	Sulfadoxine-pyrimethamine
SSD	*Service de Santé de District*/ District Health Service
UNICEF	United Nations Children's Fund
USAID	United States Agency for International Development
USG	United States Government
WHO	World Health Organization
WHOPES	WHO Pesticide Evaluation Scheme

I. EXECUTIVE SUMMARY

When it was launched in 2005, the goal of the President's Malaria Initiative (PMI) was to reduce malaria-related mortality by 50% across 15 high-burden countries in sub-Saharan Africa through a rapid scale-up of four proven and highly effective malaria prevention and treatment measures: insecticide-treated mosquito nets (ITNs); indoor residual spraying (IRS); accurate diagnosis and prompt treatment with artemisinin-based combination therapies (ACTs); and intermittent preventive treatment for pregnant women (IPTp). With the passage of the Tom Lantos and Henry J. Hyde Global Leadership against HIV/AIDS, Tuberculosis, and Malaria Act in 2008, PMI developed a U.S. Government Malaria Strategy for 2009–2014. This strategy included a long-term vision for malaria control in which sustained high coverage with malaria prevention and treatment interventions would progressively lead to malaria-free zones in Africa, with the ultimate goal of worldwide malaria eradication by 2040-2050. Consistent with this strategy and the increase in annual appropriations supporting PMI, four new sub-Saharan African countries and one regional program in the Greater Mekong Sub-region of Southeast Asia were added in 2011. The contributions of PMI, together with those of other partners, have led to dramatic improvements in the coverage of malaria control interventions in PMI-supported countries, and all 15 original countries have documented substantial declines in all-cause mortality rates among children less than five years of age.

In 2015, PMI launched the next six-year strategy, setting forth a bold and ambitious goal and objectives. The PMI Strategy 2015-2020 takes into account the progress over the past decade and the new challenges that have arisen. Malaria prevention and control remains a major U.S. foreign assistance objective and PMI's strategy fully aligns with the U.S. Government's vision of ending preventable child and maternal deaths and ending extreme poverty. It is also in line with the goals articulated in the RBM Partnership's second generation global malaria action plan, *Action and Investment to defeat Malaria (AIM) 2016-2030: for a Malaria-Free World* and WHO's updated *Global Technical Strategy: 2016-2030*. Under the PMI Strategy 2015-2020, the U.S. Government's goal is to work with PMI-supported countries and partners to further reduce malaria deaths and substantially decrease malaria morbidity, towards the long-term goal of elimination.

Madagascar was selected as a PMI focus country in December 2006, with full implementation starting in 2008. After a military coup in 2009, PMI was unable to provide direct assistance to the government of Madagascar (GoM), hindering ability to support activities at the health facility level, including support for malaria in pregnancy, case management and monitoring and evaluation activities. Nevertheless, between 2009 and 2014, PMI focused support on the Madagascar National Strategic Plan for malaria; increased efficiencies through greater coordination and programmatic integration with key partners; implemented woman- and girl-centered approaches through its community-level programming; and improved and expanded the monitoring and evaluation of the program. As a result of internationally recognized free and fair presidential elections in December 2013, the U.S. Government lifted the restrictions on working directly with the GoM health system in May 2014, and re-engaged with the GoM from the central level to the primary health facility level.

This FY 2016 Malaria Operational Plan presents a detailed implementation plan for Madagascar, based on the strategies of PMI and the National Malaria Control Program (NMCP). It was developed in consultation with the NMCP and with the participation of national and international partners involved in malaria prevention and control in the country. The activities that PMI is proposing to support fit in well with the National Strategic Plan for malaria (NSP) and build on investments made by PMI and other partners to improve and expand malaria-related services, including the Global Fund to Fight AIDS, Tuberculosis, and Malaria (Global Fund) malaria grants. This document briefly reviews the current status of malaria control policies and interventions in Madagascar, describes progress to date, identifies challenges and unmet needs to achieving the targets of the NMCP and PMI, and provides a description of activities that are planned with FY 2016 funding.

The proposed FY 2016 PMI budget for Madagascar is $26 million. PMI will support the following intervention areas with FY 2016 funds:

Insecticide-treated nets (ITNs): PMI is supporting the 2013-2017 NSP goal of universal coverage with one ITN per two persons in 92 of the 112 health districts where seasonal or perennial malaria transmission occurs. PMI supports free mass distribution campaigns to achieve equitable coverage, and is scaling up keep-up strategies, such as continuous distribution methods at the community level to replace damaged nets and cover new sleeping spaces. PMI also supports social marketing of highly subsidized ITNs in limited peri-urban areas, and with the lifting of restrictions is now supporting routine distribution in health facilities to reach pregnant women coming for antenatal care and children coming for vaccination. PMI procured 6.35 million ITNs to support the September 2015 mass distribution campaign. FY 2016 funds will be used to support routine and continuous distribution of ITNs following the ITN mass campaign.

Indoor residual spraying (IRS): The revised 2013–2017 NSP calls for focalized IRS targeting 17 low burden districts in the Central Highlands (CHL) that are stratified at the commune level and covering up to 30% of communes with highest transmission. PMI supported IRS in the CHL since 2008, and in the South since 2010, based on the national strategy. Currently, PMI is piloting IRS in some higher burden districts of the East Coast, and will add one district from the South East, where epidemiological evidence indicates transmission rates are chronically higher than expected, despite the availability of ITNs. With FY 2016 funds, PMI plans to continue piloting IRS in the East Coast and South East, and will continue to support entomological monitoring in a sample of sites throughout Madagascar, including monitoring of the residual efficacy of the insecticide class.

Malaria in pregnancy (MIP): Intermittent preventive treatment for pregnant women (IPTp) using sulfadoxine-pyrimethamine (SP) was adopted as a national policy in late 2004 in the 93 districts where stable malaria transmission occurs. Because of the political constraints related to working with Government of Madagascar since March 2009, PMI has focused its efforts to prevent and control malaria in pregnancy on behavior change communication (BCC) at the community level to promote early and frequent antenatal care (ANC) clinic attendance and improve understanding of the benefits of IPTp. With the lifting of restrictions in May 2014, PMI has re-engaged at the health facility level and is now focusing on strengthening MIP activities, including ensuring availability of SP, quinine, ACTs and ITNs for pregnant women. In FY 2015, PMI will support the NMCP revisions of IPTp policy to align them with updated WHO IPTp recommendations, and the training for a national cadre of trainers in MIP as part of comprehensive ANC service delivery. With FY 2016 funding, PMI will continue to support strengthening of MIP activities both at the community and public facility levels, and will procure approximately 500,000 treatments of SP for use at ANC.

Case management: Under the revised 2013–2017 NSP, the goal for case management is to correctly diagnose and treat at least 80% of malaria cases seen at public and private health facilities. PMI activities to improve diagnostics, supply chain management, and case management at public health facilities were suspended in FY 2009, and subsequently focused on community-based interventions and support to non-governmental organizations (NGOs) and faith-based organizations (FBOs). PMI has supported integrated community case management (iCCM) of malaria, pneumonia, and diarrhea in rural communities and has reached about half of those communities nationwide. PMI's two bilateral projects support community case management and related malaria activities in 15 regions of Madagascar; Global Fund covers the remaining seven regions, and all activities are implemented under the leadership of the NMCP. To date, PMI has supported training of more than 14,000 Community Health Volunteers (CHVs) in malaria case management. In collaboration with implementing partners, PMI has set up 1,178 malaria commodities supply points at the commune level to serve the CHVs. PMI has also supported training in malaria diagnostics and RDT use by providers from NGO/FBO run health facilities. With the lifting of restrictions, PMI supported a health facility survey to assess readiness to provide high quality care, level of support given to CHVs, and health workers' malaria case management practices. Following the assessment, PMI supported training of 18 clinicians and 16 laboratory technicians from government health facilities from 10 out of 22 regions who will serve as trainers and supervisors in malaria diagnostics and treatment. These trainers will facilitate cascade training in their respective regions, and conduct supervisory visits at designated health facilities, and establish quality assurance (QA)/ quality control (QC) programs within these facilities. In FY 2015, PMI will support the implementation of outreach diagnostic and case management training and supportive supervision (OTSS) in 40 health facilities from ten regions. PMI will provide support through bilateral projects to health facilities (HF) and 15,166 CHVs for refresher training, as well as routine supervision of CHVs by health staff. With FY 2016 funds, PMI will support refresher training, supportive supervision, and national laboratory QA/QC capacity, as well as strengthen the supply chain and distribution of malaria commodities at both the community and HF levels through the re-integration of the CHV supply chain into the national supply chain and the phase out of the parallel CHV supply chain.

Health systems strengthening and capacity building: The NMCP leads national control efforts through the formulation of policies and strategies, coordination of malaria control partners, and implementation as secondary recipients of most of the Global Fund malaria grants. Health service quality is substantially below standard, and public and non-governmental sector capacity to plan effectively and manage health programs is weak. PMI is working with the Ministry of Health (MoH) to strengthen the supply chain, in-service training and supervision, and leadership/management and governance. PMI funds contributed to multiple assessments in 2014, including assessments of the national pharmaceutical supply chain, health facility services for malaria, and a malaria KAP (Knowledge, Attitude, Practice) survey. PMI also contributed to the assessment of maternal and child health services which included findings on quality of IPTp services in health facilities. PMI will focus on building NMCP technical and managerial capacity at all levels of the health care system, both through implementing partners and direct support to the NMCP and other government partners in FY 2015. With FY 2016 funding, PMI will continue to support strengthening of the commodity supply chain, MIP and malaria case management at health facilities, and leadership/management and governance activities.

Behavior change communication (BCC): The NMCP developed the 2013-2017 BCC action plan with the overall objective of achieving 85% use of malaria prevention and case management services among the target population. PMI supports a variety of BCC strategies to promote healthy behaviors including mass- and mid-media approaches such as radio spots, mobile videos with local actors, and print materials for sensitization. PMI also supports over 14,000 CHVs in 65 districts providing interpersonal malaria BCC messages to promote correct care seeking and prevention behaviors. PMI will continue to support malaria messages reaching rural areas through community-based interpersonal communication by CHVs, skits and dramas, mobile video unit shows, and radio spots in FY 2015, and will reengage health care providers at facility level. With FY 2016 funds, PMI will continue to ensure that CHVs and health facility staff have access to and utilize BCC materials and tools that are standardized and harmonized across all malaria partner activities.

Monitoring and evaluation (M&E): The National Malaria M&E Strategy calls for the strengthening of the M&E system in order to detect and control most epidemics, and assure that at least 80% of malaria data are reported from health facilities. PMI contributed to the nationwide 2008/2009 Demographic Health Survey (DHS), the 2011 and 2013 Malaria Indicator Surveys (MIS), the 2013 Millennium Development Goal survey, and continues to provide support for fever surveillance at 15 sentinel sites collecting weekly data. PMI is working with the MoH to complete a comprehensive assessment of the national Health Management Information System (HMIS), and various disease surveillance systems. PMI will continue to support malaria survey activities including the 2016 MIS, routine data management and epidemic surveillance with FY 2015 funds. With FY 2016 funds, PMI will continue to help strengthen the national HMIS system through targeted support to the MoH for training, supportive supervision, and materials for the routine data system, and help support the integration of various surveillance systems into the Integrated Disease Surveillance and Response (IDSR) system.

Operational research (OR): The updated NMCP OR priority areas include: (1) the use of sterile mosquitoes for malaria control; (2) therapeutic efficacy studies, and; (3) anthropological studies to inform behavior change communication activities to reduce malaria burden and improve access to services. PMI is currently supporting an operational research activity to assess the effectiveness and costs of various approaches to active case detection in districts with very low transmission in the Central Highlands. The study will examine various approaches to reactive case detection around passively detected malaria cases, in order to help the NMCP determine the most feasible and effective approaches to further reduce and maintain malaria transmission at low levels. PMI will also support an anthropological study to assess ITN use and barriers in different regions of Madagascar, in order to inform the NMCP on optimal ITN BCC messages and use in FY 2015. With FY 2016 funds, PMI will support a study to inform the NMCP on reasons for delayed or non-care seeking behavior of caretakers of children and adults with fever, at the community and health facility levels.

II. STRATEGY

1. Introduction

When it was launched in 2005, the goal of PMI was to reduce malaria-related mortality by 50% across 15 high-burden countries in sub-Saharan Africa through a rapid scale-up of four proven and highly effective malaria prevention and treatment measures: insecticide-treated mosquito nets (ITNs); indoor residual spraying (IRS); accurate diagnosis and prompt treatment with artemisinin-based combination therapies (ACTs); and intermittent preventive treatment for pregnant women (IPTp). With the passage of the Tom Lantos and Henry J. Hyde Global Leadership against HIV/AIDS, Tuberculosis, and Malaria Act in 2008, PMI developed a U.S. Government Malaria Strategy for 2009–2014. This strategy included a long-term vision for malaria control in which sustained high coverage with malaria prevention and treatment interventions would progressively lead to malaria-free zones in Africa, with the ultimate goal of worldwide malaria eradication by 2040-2050. Consistent with this strategy and the increase in annual appropriations supporting PMI, four new sub-Saharan African countries and one regional program in the Greater Mekong Subregion of Southeast Asia were added in 2011. The contributions of PMI, together with those of other partners, have led to dramatic improvements in the coverage of malaria control interventions in PMI-supported countries, and all 15 original countries have documented substantial declines in all-cause mortality rates among children less than five years of age.

In 2015, PMI launched the next six-year strategy, setting forth a bold and ambitious goal and objectives. The PMI Strategy 2015-2020 takes into account the progress over the past decade and the new challenges that have risen. Malaria prevention and control remains a major U.S. foreign assistance objective and PMI's strategy fully aligns with the U.S. Government's vision of ending preventable child and maternal deaths and extreme poverty. It is also in line with the goals articulated in the RBM Partnership's second generation global malaria action plan, *Action and Investment to defeat Malaria (AIM) 2016-2030: for a Malaria-Free World* and WHO's updated *Global Technical Strategy: 2016-2030*. Under the PMI Strategy 2015-2020, the U.S. Government's goal is to work with PMI-supported countries and partners to further reduce malaria deaths and substantially decrease malaria morbidity, towards the long-term goal of elimination.

Madagascar was selected as a PMI focus country in December 2006, with full implementation starting in 2008. After a military coup in 2009, PMI was unable to provide direct assistance to the government of Madagascar (GoM), hindering ability to support activities at the health facility level, including support for malaria in pregnancy, case management and monitoring and evaluation activities. Nevertheless, between 2009 and 2014, PMI focused support on the Madagascar National Strategic Plan for malaria; increased efficiencies through greater coordination and programmatic integration with key partners; implemented woman- and girl-centered approaches through its community-level programming; and improved and expanded the monitoring and evaluation of the program. As a result of internationally recognized free and fair presidential elections in December 2013, the U.S. Government lifted the restrictions on working directly with the GoM health system in May 2014, and re-engaged with the GoM from the central level to the primary health facility level.

This FY 2016 Malaria Operational Plan presents a detailed implementation plan for Madagascar, based on the strategies of PMI and the National Malaria Control Program (NMCP). It was developed in consultation with the NMCP and with the participation of national and international partners involved in malaria prevention and control in the country. The activities that PMI is proposing to support fit in well with the National Malaria Control strategy and plan and build on investments made by PMI and other partners to improve and expand malaria-related services, including the Global Fund to Fight AIDS, Tuberculosis, and Malaria (Global Fund) malaria grants. This document briefly reviews the current status of malaria control policies and interventions in Madagascar, describes progress to date, identifies challenges and unmet needs to achieving the targets of the NMCP and PMI, and provides a description of activities that are planned with FY 2016 funding.

2. Malaria situation in Madagascar

Malaria is endemic in 90% of Madagascar; however the entire population is considered to be at risk for the disease. Malaria cases and deaths reported through the national Health Management Information System (HMIS) have fallen between 2003 and 2013. Among all age groups, malaria morbidity decreased from 19% in 2003 to 6.5% in 2013, and from 21.6% in 2003 to 6.8% in 2013 among children under five years of age. In 2013, malaria was the eighth leading cause of morbidity among children under five, down from second in 2007, and the second leading cause of death among children under five in 2013 as reported by district hospitals.[1] While hospital deaths attributed to malaria fell from 17% in 2003 to 10% in 2012, severe malaria remained among the top five causes of reported overall mortality.[2]

Madagascar witnessed a decade of health improvement between 1997 and 2008. According to the 2009 Demographic and Health Survey (DHS), under-five mortality fell from 159 per 1,000 live births in 1997 to 72[3] and 62[4] per 1,000 live births by 2008 and 2012 respectively. Other determinants of child survival — such as morbidity and coverage of important health interventions — have improved significantly during this period. For instance, between 1997 and 2008, the prevalence of diarrhea in children decreased by about 70% and respiratory infections by approximately 87%, while the proportion of moderately or severely anemic children fell by 59% between 1997 and 2008.

Despite these improvements in child health indicators, Madagascar still faces major health challenges, which threaten social and economic development. Access to and quality of health services have been negatively impacted by the political crisis, which started with the March 2009 coup and led to more than 200 primary health center (*centre de santé de base* - CSB) closures over the last six years. National health infrastructure, information, and commodity management systems are extremely weak, and much remains to be done at central and regional levels to ensure quality services and sustainable health financing.

These challenges have a significant impact on overall health and malaria activities at every level of the public health system. There have been delays in planned health policy reform, limited supervisory and monitoring visits due to security issues and lack of funds, delayed data reporting, and interruptions in supplies of essential medicines to the health facility level. The

---

[1] Annuaire Statistique 2013
[2] NSP 2013-2017
[3] DHS 2009 Report
[4] MDG Survey Report 2013

nongovernmental sector has reported difficulties due to insecurity in the field and reduced capacity of the health sector at the decentralized level as a result of changes in personnel and delays in fund disbursements. With the lifting of restrictions, and a new MoH leadership, there are plans to reopen more than 100 CSBs by June 2015, recruit 300 new personnel for CSBs by September 2015, and strengthen the supply chain to provide access to commodities all the way down to the CSB level.

The country has been stratified into four malaria epidemiologic zones based on the duration and intensity of malaria transmission: the East Coast; the West Coast including the North; the Central Highlands; and the South, roughly corresponding to the bioclimatic map below. The rainy season varies, starting in late October or early November and lasts until April or May; however, on the East Coast the rainy season and increased malaria transmission may last as long as nine months. The cyclone season extends from December to April. In February 2015, Cyclone Chedza hit Madagascar, resulting in widespread devastation and destruction of homes and property in the southeast and the Central Highlands, including the capital city Antananarivo. Cyclone Chedza caused flooding, landslides, displacement of populations, and increased risk of communicable diseases and malaria, compounded by the loss of ITNs.

Figure 1: Madagascar Malariometric Stratification

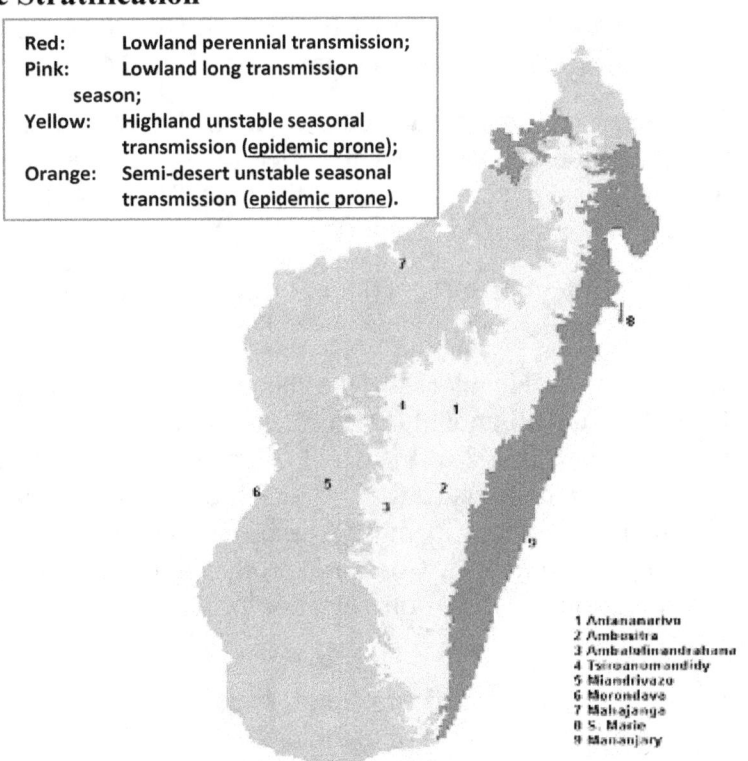

The East Coast has perennial transmission and the West Coast has seasonal transmission that typically runs from October to May with reduced transmission in July and August. In both regions, immunity among adults is reported to be high and most morbidity and mortality is among children under five years of age and pregnant women. Almost one-third of the Central Highlands lies above 1,500 meters, where malaria transmission does not occur, or the transmission season is short, seasonal, and unstable. In the semi-desert South, transmission is also seasonal but very unstable and in some areas, is almost absent. Immunity is limited in the human population of both the upper Central Highlands (CHL) and the South, and those areas are prone to periodic epidemics, which are often associated with high levels of mortality in all age groups. The most recent large-scale epidemic occurred in the late 1980s in the Central Highlands and killed an estimated 30,000 people. The Fringe districts of the CHL are those areas with an altitude between 800 and 900 meters that lie between the epidemic-prone areas of the upper CHL and the malaria-endemic areas on the coasts.

Plasmodium falciparum is the predominant species of malaria parasite in all areas. The 2013 Malaria Indicator Survey (MIS) found less than 1% of *P. vivax* and *P. malariae*. However, historically the prevalence of non-*Plasmodium falciparum* infections has been higher in certain epidemiological zones. A 2007 study showed that among 709 randomly selected school age children seen at eight sites throughout the country, the prevalence of each *Plasmodium* species was 16.2% *P. falciparum*, 13.0% *P. vivax*, 3.6% *P. ovale*, and 1.8% *P. malariae*; 5.2% of participants were infected[5]. The two primary vectors are *Anopheles gambiae* s.l. (East and West Coasts) and *An. funestus* (CHL and South). *An. arabiensis* is present in all four epidemiological zones. *An. funestus* increases in abundance during the rice-growing season and was the primary vector responsible for the outbreaks in the CHL in the late 1980s. Since this vector prefers to feed and rest indoors, it is quite sensitive to indoor residual spraying (IRS). *An. arabiensis*, also present in the Central Highlands, is more ecologically independent of humans and their domestic environment. *An. mascarensis* has been reported as a primary vector in the southeast and as a secondary vector on the island district of Sainte Marie.

The revised NSP has organized the country into two malaria operational zones based on changes in transmission dynamics, local epidemiology, and level of coverage of malaria interventions: the high transmission zone, including the East Coast and West Coast, and the low transmission zone including the South, and the CHL.

3. Country health system delivery structure and Ministry of Health (MoH) organization

The Ministry of Health (MoH) at the national level is represented by the cabinet of the Minister of Health and the national directorates reporting directly to the Director General for Health under the Secretary General of the MoH. Madagascar is administratively divided into 22 regions, 119 administrative districts (only 112 health districts), 1,579 communes, and 17,500 *fokontany*,[6] the equivalent of villages in most African countries. Each region has a regional health directorate and a regional hospital. Contrary to other administrators in Madagascar, the *fokontany* chief is chosen through a grass roots selection process by community members and is not affiliated with a political party.

The organization of the health system follows the same general organization as the administrative system down to the district level. At the commune level there is at least one public primary health care facility (CSB), serving each commune. The formal health system is composed of four levels[7]:

- There are six university teaching hospitals in the capital city and five former provinces, plus 10 specialized referral centers

---

[5] http://www.pnas.org/content/107/13/5967 full.pdf
[6] INSTAT, 2012
[7] Annuaire des Statistiques du Secteur Sante 2012

- There are 16 regional hospitals for patients requiring a higher level of care that serve as tertiary care health facilities
- There are 87 first referral district public hospitals
- There are 2,563 CSBs. Among these, 1,616 are known as CSB Level II, which are expected to be staffed with at least one physician, and 947 CSB Level I, which are staffed by a nurse or paramedic and in some cases a nurse's aide.

In addition, about 630 health facilities are privately run, predominantly by non-governmental organizations (NGO)/faith-based organizations (FBOs). The majority of these facilities are classified as CSBs. Since 2012, PMI supports training and donation of malaria commodities, mostly RDTs, in 161 NGO/FBO run facilities offering malaria diagnostics and treatment services. Some FBO-run hospitals are part of the district level hospitals[1].

The MoH has a critical staff shortage at all levels of the public health system, especially for service provision below the central level. In addition, health workers are not distributed equitably throughout the country, resulting in higher concentrations of qualified health staff in the urban areas. According to the 2013 National Health Statistics (*Annuaire des Statistiques du Secteur Santé*), the national ratio of doctors to the population is 1 per 6,200, with rural regions having less than one doctor for every 10,000 inhabitants.

Regional and District heads oversee health teams that implement integrated health interventions; currently all regional and district health teams have malaria focal persons. The District Hospital is the first referral structure for CSBs; the district health team, currently known as *service de santé de district* is headed by a medical chief called *Médécin Inspecteur*, responsible for technical supervision of all CSBs in his/her jurisdiction.

The malaria control unit was established in 1921 with the aim of preventing malaria epidemics. Until the late 1980s, the focus was on the 26 epidemic-prone districts. In 1998, the first five-year national malaria control strategy was designed, defining control interventions per transmission zones and introducing the use of chloroquine for community-based malaria treatment and chemoprophylaxis among pregnant women. In June 2011, the GoM elevated the malaria control service to a National Malaria Control Program (NMCP) directorate level in the MoH organizational structure. Assisted by a Deputy Director, the NMCP Director supervises a team comprising six technical divisions: Vector Control, Case Management, Laboratory, Epidemiologic Surveillance, M&E, and BCC, and one support division: Finance and Administration. With the June 2014 Government Decree restructuring the organization of the MoH, the NMCP was elevated to the cabinet level, under direct supervision of the Minister. A recent government decree (February 2015) repositioned the Program back under direct supervision of the Director General for Health. The program was renamed *Direction de la Lutte contre le Paludisme (DLP)*.

In 2008, Madagascar approved an integrated community case management (iCCM) package offered by Community Health Volunteers (CHVs) to deliver health services at the fokontany level. Currently, CHVs provide treatment for children under five diagnosed with uncomplicated malaria, acute respiratory infections, and diarrhea. They also offer family planning for eligible families, micronutrient supplementation, and nutrition monitoring and referral. The community-based health services policy calls for a more comprehensive package of services including primary care to newborns for CHVs. Three recent pilots, one testing the administration of pregnancy test kits, a second testing the prevention of postpartum hemorrhage by the distribution of misoprostol by CHVs, and a third testing newborn infection prevention using chlorhexidine by CHVs were successful and are being scaled up. Based on the national implementation directives, each *fokontany* has a team of two CHVs, one specialized in child health and another in maternal and reproductive health. Plans are underway to cross-train all CHVs so that they can at least advise and refer all maternal and child patients in their respective communities. There are over 34,000 CHVs in the country, trained mostly by a Global Fund National Strategy Application (NSA) grant and by the United States Agency for International Development (USAID)-funded integrated bilateral health projects.

The iCCM package through CHVs is supported by USAID-funded projects and targets populations in *fokontanys* located five kilometers or more than one hour's walk from the nearest health facility. However, the selection and establishment of CHVs supported by Global Fund is not based on the same distance criteria. Harmonization of the two approaches will be undertaken soon. In addition, three directorates in the MoH — *DLP*, Maternal Child and Reproductive Health, and the Health Districts Directorate —share responsibility for the oversight of the iCCM activities, which makes coordination and ownership a challenge. Especially challenging are harmonization of supervision tools and content, commodity management, activity reporting, and data management. Both Global Fund and USAID are actively engaged to support the establishment of integrated systems.

4. National malaria control strategy

The 2013–2017 National Strategic Plan (NSP) for malaria was updated in December 2014, following a midterm review. It was determined that based on 2014 health facility data, progress towards pre-elimination targets was slow and many districts' routine data showed an increase in malaria burden. The negative impact of the political crisis, the interruption of many activities for more than two years under Global Fund, and the limits to the NMCP capacity as secondary recipient in implementing activities under Global Fund grants were identified as major causes of slow progress. The revised strategy has reorganized the country into two main malaria control zones based on changes in transmission dynamics, local epidemiology, and level of coverage of malaria interventions: the high transmission zone, including the East Coast and the West Coast, and the low transmission zone including the South, the CHL, and Fringe areas.

Insecticide-treated nets (ITNs): In 2008, a major strategic change regarding ITN distribution in Madagascar occurred, moving from targeted distribution of ITNs to vulnerable groups, to universal coverage defined in the 2008–2012 National Strategy as two nets per household in 92 malaria endemic districts, and excluding the 20 CHL districts mostly covered by IRS and epidemic surveillance systems. Under the 2013-2017 National Strategy, the ITN universal coverage goal was redefined to align with WHO and Alliance for Malaria Prevention recommendation of one net per two persons. By the end of 2015, the goal is for at least 80% of households in targeted districts to own at least one ITN per two persons. Madagascar prioritizes free ITN distribution through mass campaigns as the primary approach to scaling up to universal coverage. In addition, three "keep up" strategies are supported: routine distribution through antenatal care (ANC) and expanded program on immunization (EPI) clinics; continuous distribution in endemic districts through CHVs aiming to cover every sleeping space and replace damaged or lost nets; and the sale of highly subsidized ITNs in some peri-urban communities.

Indoor residual spraying (IRS): The 2013–2017 NSP calls for focalized IRS stratified by commune in three geographic zones, which have completed three to four consecutive years of blanket IRS: the CHL; the Fringe areas bordering the CHL; and districts to the west and south of the Fringe. Blanket IRS was coupled with free mass ITN distribution in 2010 and 2013 in all except the CHL districts. At the end of the 2011 spray round, the CHL and Fringe districts completed four consecutive years of universal IRS coverage and transitioned to focalized spraying. By the end of the 2012 spray round, the extension districts to the South and West had received three consecutive years of blanket IRS coverage and the majority of districts transitioned to focalized IRS, except for the districts in the South. Focalized IRS includes only the highest transmission communes and relies on malaria surveillance and response planning to prevent epidemics. Approximately 30% of all communes undergo spraying, which is prioritized based on clinical and entomological data that show the highest levels of ongoing transmission. Following revisions of the IRS strategy in December 2014, Madagascar has now limited IRS to 17 districts in the CHL not covered by mass ITN distribution. The decision was made after careful review of household survey findings which showed no significant added value of combining IRS with ITNs in low transmission districts. The country is also piloting IRS in three Eastern districts and a Southeast district to measure transmission impact of coupling IRS and ITNs in high burden areas.

Malaria in pregnancy (MIP): Intermittent preventive treatment for pregnant women (IPTp) has been implemented since 2004 and currently covers 93 endemic districts where malaria transmission is stable or seasonal, and excludes 19 CHL districts. The MIP strategy includes the provision and promotion of ITN use during pregnancy and IPTp, delivered as a package during ANC visits. The 2013–2017 National Strategic Plan was recently updated to providing sulfadoxine-pyrimethamine (SP) at each ANC visit after quickening, in order to align with WHO's recent recommendation on new SP dosing during pregnancy. Administration of IPTp should be directly observed and free-of-charge. CHVs play an essential role in promoting the use of antenatal services. All focused antenatal care, including tetanus vaccination and malaria prevention activities, is integrated at the CSB level. The NMCP works closely with the *Direction de la Santé Familiale –Directorate of Family Health (*former *Direction de la Santé de l'Enfant, de la Mère et de la Reproduction)* to plan and implement MIP activities, including IPTp. The NMCP has also included IPTp as part of an integrated ANC services package during the mother and child health promotion weeks held twice a year in April and October. In addition to ANC counseling, these biannual health weeks include other health focused activities such as the distribution of vitamin A and deworming medicines to children 6–59 months, and iron, and folic acid to pregnant women, implementation of mass immunization campaigns, and dissemination of health promotion messages.

Case management: ACTs were adopted as the first-line treatment for malaria in 2005. ACTs and RDTs were rolled out in public health facilities from late 2006 through 2008 and at the community level in late 2008. The NMCP policy requires that, where possible, all cases of malaria be diagnosed by microscopy or RDT, including at the community level. Where biological diagnosis is not possible, diagnosis should be based on clinical evaluation and treatment should be provided after other causes of fever have been excluded. Under the revised 2013–2017 National Strategic Plan, the goal for case management is to correctly diagnose and treat at least 80% of malaria cases seen at public and private health facilities. First-line treatment is artesunate-amodiaquine (AS/AQ) (except for pregnant women in their first trimester, in which case treatment is oral quinine); in the six pre-elimination districts in the CHL within the low transmission zone, the national strategy also calls for administration of a single low dose of primaquine in addition to AS/AQ for cases of simple malaria, except in pregnant women and children less than four years of age. Treatment of severe malaria is parenteral artesunate at the hospital level. Rectal artesunate should be administered as a pre-referral treatment at community and health facility levels for symptoms of severe malaria in children less than five years of age. As of early 2015, injectable artesunate and pre-referral rectal artesunate had not yet been rolled out, but this is planned to occur before the end of 2015.

Health systems strengthening (HSS): The NMCP leads national control efforts through the formulation of policies and strategies, coordination of malaria control partners, and implementation as secondary recipient of the majority of Global Fund malaria grants. Health service quality is substantially below standard, and the NMCP capacity to plan effectively, implement efficiently, and report on time is limited. Additional challenges for the NMCP include ensuring effective coordination from the central level down to the district level with other government directorates who have equal responsibility in disease control, epidemiological surveillance, program oversight and reporting, and training and supervision of staff who lack skills in malaria control. The November 2014 strategy review adopted decentralization principles with the plan to give more responsibility to regional and district teams in management of human and financial resources. The revised strategy also adopted the integration of malaria commodities management into the MoH logistics and commodity management unit.

Monitoring and evaluation (M&E): The 2013–2017 National Malaria M&E Strategy calls for the strengthening of the M&E system in order to detect and control 100% of epidemics, and assure the quality of at least 80% of data reported from health facilities on malaria. The revised strategy set the objective of ensuring availability of quality epidemiological data to make it possible to monitor the evolution of malaria across the transmission zones. The strategy supports the adoption of the web-based District Health Information System2 (DHIS2) to improve access to data and integrate multiple existing health data management systems. The strategy also supports the expansion of SMS messaging to improve epidemic surveillance and completeness of reporting from remote and inaccessible districts. NMCP plans to strengthen the integrated HMIS system and the Integrated Disease Surveillance and Response (IDSR) system.

Operational research (OR): The NMCP Operational Research priorities are linked to major malaria control interventions supported by PMI. The November 2014 midterm review of the 2103–2017 national strategy listed the following OR priority areas for the remaining time of the strategy: (1) the use of sterile mosquitoes for malaria control; (2) therapeutic efficacy studies; and (3) anthropological studies to inform behavior change communication activities, in association with malaria burden and access to services.

Behavior change communication (BCC): The NMCP developed the 2013–2017 BCC action plan with the overall objective of achieving 85% use of malaria prevention and case management services among the target population. The November 2014 strategy review put an emphasis on mobilizing mothers and care givers to seek prompt treatment for children with fever within 24 hours, and priority to regionalized BCC design, using anthropologic study findings. The strategy plans to improve public relations and advocacy, mobilize decision makers and communities, increase interpersonal communication, and enhance service providers' skills in communicating with care seekers.

The table below describes the key strategies by transmission zone.

Table 1: NMCP Strategy by Intervention and Transmission Zone

Strategies/interventions	High Transmission Control Zones (endemic East and West)	Low Transmission control zones (non-endemic CHL, Fringes and South)
IRS		
Focalized IRS		√ (17 districts in CHL)
Focalized IRS for epidemic response	√	√
ITNs		
ITN universal coverage	√	√ (South and Fringes)
Routine and continuous ITN distribution	√	√ (South and Fringes)
Focalized ITN distribution in response to epidemics	√	√ (South and Fringes)
IPTp		
IPTp among pregnant women	√	√ (South and Fringes)
Case management		
Diagnostic case confirmation	√	√
ACTs for confirmed cases	√	√
Radical treatment (ACT plus primaquine) for confirmed cases		√ (CHL)
Surveillance		
Weekly surveillance	√	√
(Re)active case detection during an epidemic (ACTs for confirmed cases)	√	
(Re)active case detection, around an index case (ACT + PQ for confirmed		√ (6 districts in CHL)

5. Updates in the strategy section

The November 2014 midterm review of the 2013–2017 NSP led to a revision of the program objectives and a reclassification of transmission zones into control zones of high and low transmission, moving away from the previously identified three geographic zones: control, consolidation, and pre-elimination zones. The revision was based on household survey findings and a review of routine data from health facilities. Intervention strategies are now being implemented according to the new operational stratification taking into account the vulnerability of districts with a focus on key populations. Among the major changes to the strategy as mentioned earlier are the adoption of focalized IRS only in low transmission districts in the CHL, and the phased implementation of the new WHO guidelines on IPTp.

6. Integration, collaboration, and coordination

Several donors and partners support malaria interventions in Madagascar, including PMI, Global Fund, United Nations Children's Fund (UNICEF), WHO, and Roll Back Malaria (RBM)/Southern Africa Regional Network, with the NMCP coordinating all partners. Under NMCP leadership, a strong local RBM partnership has been established, and committee meetings are held monthly. Over the last five years, RBM partners worked closely to oversee and conduct two Malaria Indicator Surveys (MIS 2011 and MIS 2013), to plan and design the Malaria Program Review (July 2011), to organize and facilitate a national conference on pre-elimination (November 2011) to inform the design of the 2013–2017 National Strategic Plan, to conduct the 2012 and 2013 mass distribution of over nine million ITNs in 92 districts, and to coordinate technical assistance as needed at all levels. More recently, in November 2014, RBM partners conducted a midterm review of the 2013–2017 National Strategic Plan, resulting in setting new targets for some of the major malaria control measures. Currently, RBM partners are preparing an ITN mass distribution campaign planned for September /October 2015 covering all the 92 targeted districts.

With FY 2016 funding, PMI will continue to seek opportunities to collaborate with other USG health programs to ensure maximum impact for every health dollar the USG invests in the country. PMI has been supporting the integration of maternal and child health services at the community level since 2009. Since malaria prevention and control activities have been implemented as part of integrated maternal and child health services, PMI will contribute to strengthen the capacity to deliver these services. PMI will work with other USG-funded programs and other partners to support the comprehensive primary health care package, including the training and implementation of community-based diagnosis and treatment of fever, early correct case management, and IPTp.

7. PMI goal, objectives, strategic areas, and key indicators

Under the PMI Strategy for 2015-2020, the U.S. Government's goal is to work with PMI-supported countries and partners to further reduce malaria deaths and substantially decrease malaria morbidity, towards the long-term goal of elimination. Building upon the progress to date in PMI-supported countries, PMI will work with NMCPs and partners to accomplish the following objectives by 2020:

1. Reduce malaria mortality by one-third from 2015 levels in PMI-supported countries, achieving a greater than 80% reduction from PMI's original 2000 baseline levels.

2. Reduce malaria morbidity in PMI-supported countries by 40% from 2015 levels.

3. Assist at least five PMI-supported countries to meet the World Health Organization's (WHO) criteria for national or sub-national pre-elimination.[8]

These objectives will be accomplished by emphasizing five core areas of strategic focus:

1. Achieving and sustaining scale of proven interventions
2. Adapting to changing epidemiology and incorporating new tools
3. Improving countries' capacity to collect and use information
4. Mitigating risk against the current malaria control gains
5. Building capacity and health systems towards full country ownership

To track progress toward achieving and sustaining scale of proven interventions (area of strategic focus #1), PMI will continue to track the key indicators recommended by the Roll Back Malaria Monitoring and Evaluation Reference Group (RBM MERG) as listed below:

- Proportion of households with at least one ITN
- Proportion of households with at least one ITN for every two people
- Proportion of children under five years old who slept under an ITN the previous night
- Proportion of pregnant women who slept under an ITN the previous night
- Proportion of households in targeted districts protected by IRS
- Proportion of children under five years old with fever in the last two weeks for whom advice or treatment was sought
- Proportion of children under five with fever in the last two weeks who had a finger or heel stick
- Proportion receiving an ACT among children under five years old with fever in the last two weeks who received any antimalarial drugs
- Proportion of women who received two or more doses of IPTp for malaria during ANC visits during their last pregnancy

8. Progress on coverage/impact indicators to date

The most recent Demographic and Health Survey (DHS) was carried out from November 2008 to August 2009 and provides baseline indicators for PMI in Madagascar. Child mortality was estimated at 72 per 1,000 live births by the direct method. A Millennium Development Goal (MDG) survey was conducted in December 2012/January 2013 and estimated child mortality at 62 per 1,000 live births, a small decrease from 2009. However, maternal mortality remained high (479 deaths per 100,000 live births), and stagnated at levels similar to what was measured in the 2008/2009 DHS (498 deaths per 100,000 live births). Additional household surveys carried out include the Malaria Indicator Surveys (MIS) in 2011 and 2013. Supplementary data, including routine malaria-specific health management information system (HMIS) data and malaria program data compiled by the NMCP, are reported and centrally stored in a national malaria database. Some national malaria indicators have been estimated based on these data and

---

[8] http://whqlibdoc.who.int/publications/2007/9789241596084_eng.pdf

additional sources such as special studies and limited surveys. Results for some malaria indicators are summarized in the tables below.

Table 2: Evolution of Key Malaria Indicators in Madagascar from 2008 to 2013

Indicator	2008/09 DHS (PMI baseline)	2011 MIS	2013 MIS
% Households with at least one ITN[1]	73	94	79
% Households with at least one ITN for every two people[1]	23	40	35
% Children under five who slept under an ITN the previous night[1]	58	89	71
% Pregnant women who slept under an ITN the previous night[1]	58	85	68
% Households in targeted districts protected by IRS	N/A[2]	79[3]	59[4]
% Children under five years old with fever in the last two weeks for whom advice or treatment was sought	41	34	44
% Children under five with fever in the last two weeks who had a finger or heel stick	N/A[5]	6	15
% Children receiving an ACT among children under five years old with fever in the last two weeks who received any antimalarial drugs	5	19	54
% Women who received two or more doses of IPTp during their last pregnancy in the last two years[6]	8	22	21

[1]Among 92 targeted districts that receive ITNs per the national strategy 2008-2012
[2]The DHS 2008/2009 did not collect information on IRS
[3]Among 53 targeted health districts that benefit from IRS per the national strategy 2008-2012
[4] In 2012 Madagascar transitioned from district-wide to focalized IRS targeting communes in the Central Highlands, but the MIS estimate is at the district level.
[5]The DHS 2008/2009 did not collect information on finger/heel stick
[6]Among 93 targeted districts that benefit from IPTp

9. Other relevant evidence on progress

Household survey: A major cross-sectional study conducted in 2012 and 2013 by a local implementer to evaluate the efficacy and impact of malaria interventions collected blood samples and administered household questionnaires to 15,465 participants in 62 sites throughout the country[9]. Results from the study found that 3.7% of participants were RDT-positive, and that ITNs had a protective effect on the population. However, the study also showed that combining ITNs and IRS in low-transmission zones had no significant added value, and that the protective effect of IRS in low-transmission areas was still questionable.

Health facility survey: A nationally representative cross-sectional cluster survey of 65 outpatient public health facilities conducted in Oct-Dec 2014 showed that only 38% of health facility staff were trained to perform either malaria microscopy or RDTs. When assessed individually, 41.6% of health workers (HW) reported receiving formal training on RDT use, with the same proportion receiving formal training on malaria case management with emphasis on ACT use. A significant proportion of facilities (between 65.0% and 81.3%) had the various AS/AQ treatment courses in stock the day of the survey, but only an average of 10% of the facilities had a minimum of 20 courses on hand. Only approximately two-thirds of surveyed facilities had a copy of the national malaria control policy and just over half had a copy of the national ACT guidelines. The survey also found that HW tested 97.4% of patients for whom malaria was suspected, and that HW administered or prescribed ACTs to 86.1% of patients diagnosed with uncomplicated malaria. Weighted analysis shows that the proportion of patients diagnosed with uncomplicated malaria who were properly counseled on use of LLINs (32.3%), who returned to the HF if signs of severity were present or symptoms worsened (19.4%), who returned to the HF for a follow-up visit after two days (32.3%), who completed treatment courses to the end (23.7%), and who continued to eat while sick was relatively low. Only approximately two-thirds of HFs supervised their CHVs and provided or delivered supplies to them.

10. Challenges and opportunities

The 2009-2014 political crisis limited the USG and major international external donors from supporting health programs in the public health sector. Inadequate supervision, lack of refresher training, staffing shortages, incomplete and inaccurate reporting, and commodity stockouts have continued to pose challenges for the delivery of public health services and for the national malaria control program. Among challenges mentioned in the November 2014 midterm review of the national strategy are: 1) increased poverty (92% of the population is now living on less than two dollars a day), lack of public authority, and non-optimal implementation of malaria activities all resulting from the crisis and reduced funding; 2) insecurity in the South and the South West, further limiting implementation of malaria control programs in those areas; 3) the NMCP's limited capacity to plan and implement activities due to a weakened health system as evidenced by over 200 closed health facilities; 4) limited health data reporting in the entire health system and; 5) interruption of major activities under the Global Fund NSA II grant, leading to periods of malaria commodities stockouts including ACTs, SP, and insecticides for IRS, commodities initially planned for procurement under Global Fund.

---

[9] http://www.malariajournal.com/content/13/1/465

Following the successful presidential and legislative elections in December 2013, international donors resumed direct support to the government of Madagascar in the first semester of 2014, and the USG lifted restrictions in May 2014. With the resumption of support to the public health sector, PMI is directly engaging and collaborating with the NMCP in the implementation of the 2013-2017 National Strategic Plan. More specifically, PMI is providing technical assistance to strengthen NMCP capacity to plan and coordinate inputs from various malaria partners. An estimated 50–60% of the population does not seek care in health facilities when they are ill; some rely on self-treatment with drugs purchased illegally. Other factors limiting the use of health facilities include long distances or physical barriers such as crossing rivers in order to reach the nearest health facility, and lack of monetary income to pay for health services. At the implementation level, PMI is supporting the districts and CSB health teams to increase supervision of CHVs' work and re-engage efforts to strengthen health facility services, including training and supervision of health care staff and ensuring availability of malaria commodities.

Two parallel but complementary supply chain systems exist in Madagascar: one for the public sector and the other for socially marketed products. Highly subsidized sales of health commodities through social marketing have been promoted historically in Madagascar with funding both from the Global Fund as well as the USG. However, weak commodity management, frequent delays due to late financing from donors, and inadequate stock management and information systems lead to stockouts. PMI and partners are coordinating efforts to improve supply chain management and strengthen Madagascar's Central Medical Stores (SALAMA), the national entity in charge of procurement and distribution of medical and pharmaceutical commodities.

Lastly, the health management information system (HMIS) does not generate needed information to inform programming; routine and surveillance data reporting is neither complete nor timely and is of variable quality. Although 34,000 CHVs had been trained in community case management by December 2012, the current HMIS database does not include community health data. Future PMI support will focus on efforts to strengthen an integrated national HMIS with the aim of establishing a functional web based data management system.

III. OPERATIONAL PLAN

PMI supports all elements of the NMCP's national strategy. Along with USAID Family Planning and Maternal Child Health funding, PMI supports integrated community case management in 15 out of 22 regions through two community health bilateral projects, six regions in the hard to reach districts in the West and North, and nine regions in the West, Central and East of the country. Following the re-engagement with the GOM in May 2014, the bilateral projects are working with District Health teams to plan and implement refresher training, providers' supervision including supervision of CHVs by CSB staff, and to improve data collection and reporting. The choice of the 15 regions was a concerted effort among Madagascar health partners; the remaining 7 regions are receiving similar support from Global Fund. Since 2014, PMI has proposed a geographic refocus for IRS by piloting IRS in a few high burden districts for two to three years, to assess the impact of combining IRS and LLINs. The PMI targeted area was selected by in-country stakeholders due to its high malaria burden, despite universal LLIN coverage.

Figure 2: PMI-supported CHVs in two USAID bilateral projects

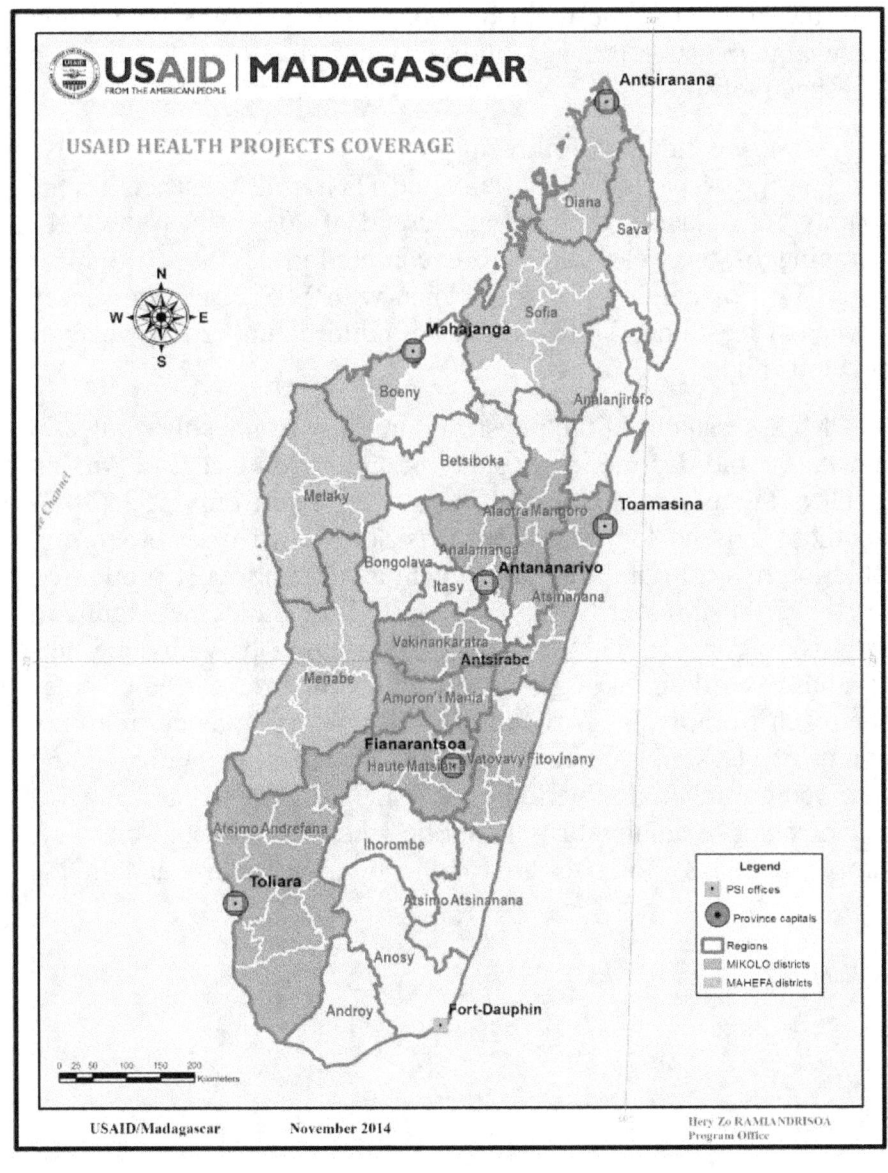

1. Insecticide-treated nets

NMCP/PMI objectives

Under the 2013–2017 National Strategic Plan, Madagascar has adopted one ITN for every two persons to achieve universal coverage for all districts in the high transmission zone, including the East Coast and the West Coast, and low transmission districts in the South and Fringe areas. There are presently six districts in the CHL meeting pre-elimination criteria; the NMCP is currently putting in place all measures necessary to declare them the starting malaria pre-elimination districts in Madagascar.

Progress since PMI was launched

Madagascar completed nationwide, mass campaigns to deliver free ITNs to reach all persons living in malaria endemic areas in 2009–2010 and again in 2012–2013. The 2009–2010 campaign achieved an average of 1.8 ITNs per household compared to the then national target of two ITNs per household according to MIS 2011[10]. This resulted in high ownership with 94%[11] of households reporting ownership of at least one ITN six months after the campaign compared to 73% ownership in 2008–2009.[12] These results were similar by geographic zone, household economic status, and households with and without children under five years of age. Furthermore, 82% of all individuals sleeping in the household the night before the survey reported sleeping under an ITN and there was even higher usage among children under five years of age and pregnant women (89% and 85% respectively).

The 2012 and 2013 mass campaigns were conducted following the earlier strategy of two ITNs per household (equating to about 1 ITN: 2.4 persons) and delivered ITNs to 31 districts on the East Coast in 2012 and the remaining 61 endemic districts at the end of 2013. Since the 2013 MIS was conducted at the beginning of the year and before completion of the 2013 mass campaign in the rest of the country, ITN ownership was lower than with MIS 2011; the survey found that 79% of households owned at least one ITN, with 71% of children under five years of age sleeping under an ITN the previous night.[13]

Several reports, including a 2012 PMI assessment of the physical durability of nets distributed in late 2009 on the East Coast, indicate a rapid decline in net survivorship in Madagascar. Among 500 polyester and polyethylene ITNs tagged and examined three years later, only 152 (30%) remained in the households. Of those nets no longer present it is not known what proportion were lost due to attrition unrelated to physical durability (e.g. given away) and what proportion were no longer present due to loss of physical integrity. Among the 152 remaining nets found in households after three years, 80% were considered "serviceable". Surviving polyethylene nets were found to have larger-sized holes overall and a larger estimated mean surface area of holes than polyester nets. Based on the result from this assessment, PMI is supporting a net durability monitoring study of the three brands of ITNs distributed during the 2013 mass campaigns in 61 districts. Three thousand ITNs are being tracked and periodic assessments of three indicators of ITN durability are being carried out: survivorship/attrition, fabric integrity, and bio-efficacy. These assessments are being implemented at six sites in rural and urban areas, and in the

---

[10] MIS 2011
[11] Madagascar 2013 Post campaign evaluation
[12] DHS 2008/9
[13] MIS 2013

different malaria transmission zones. Results will allow the NMCP of Madagascar and its partners to better define the serviceable life of an ITN in the Madagascar setting, thereby better informing program decision making around timing of distribution and replacement of ITNs.

The 2012 ITN durability assessment highlighted the need to support delivery of ITNs between campaigns to maintain high coverage. Two channels have been traditionally used in Madagascar to deliver ITNs between campaigns: delivery through routine ANC and EPI clinics and social marketing. Both were limited by net availability and far too few nets have been delivered to effectively or equitably cover the anticipated yearly ITN losses across the general population. In 2014, PMI/Madagascar tested a continuous distribution model by CHVs to improve availability of ITNs free-of-charge for households in need. CHVs visited families in their *fokontanys* and recorded needs of ITNs for pregnant women, vaccinated children, and for new and existing uncovered sleeping spaces on an as-needed basis. The model was successful in increasing availability and use of ITNs in the Toamasina II District; it is being scaled up starting with the South-Eastern districts. PMI also distributed ITNs to communities in response to epidemics or disasters, such as cyclones. Out of a stock of 27,000 ITNs set aside for cyclone and disaster response, PMI provided 8,000 nets in early 2015 to the South-Eastern region hardest hit by cyclones and resulting flooding. The current channels supported by PMI in Madagascar are listed in Table 3.

Progress during the last 12-18 months

With a combination of FY 2013 and FY 2014 funds, PMI procured 6.35 million ITNs to support a mass distribution campaign planned for September/October 2015 covering 50 districts primarily on the East Coast, the North, and North-West of the country. Part of the ITNs (1.45 million nets) have arrived in-country and are stored in a central warehouse while the remaining 4.9 million will be delivered between April and May 2015. In addition, Global Fund procured 4.2 million ITNs to cover 42 districts in the Fringes, the South, and South-West. This is the first time Madagascar is planning to conduct a mass distribution covering all 92 targeted ITN districts over a period of two months. The last two mass distribution campaigns were conducted in November/December 2012 and September/October 2013, following the 2009 and 2010 mass campaigns. The 2012 and 2013 campaigns applied the existing national policy of two ITNs per household, or the equivalent of one ITN per 2.4 persons. The upcoming campaign will follow the current national policy of one net per two persons (estimated as one ITN per 1.8 persons). PMI and Global Fund are coordinating the preparation of the campaign through improved enumeration in order to minimize risk of stockouts or low inventory at distribution sites during the campaign. The 2015 mass distribution campaign will be rolled out as shown in Figure 3.

Table 3: Madagascar national ITN distribution strategies

Type of ITN Distribution	Strategy	Approach	Target Population
Free Distribution	Catch-Up	Mass Campaign	One ITN per two persons in 92 lowland and coastal districts
	Keep-Up	Facility-based delivery to pregnant women at ANC visits to and vaccinated children at EPI visits	Pregnant women and vaccinated children in 93 lowland and coastal districts
	Keep-Up	Delivery to pregnant women and vaccinated children at community level by CHVs	Pregnant women and vaccinated children in 93 lowland and coastal districts
	Keep-Up	Community-based continuous distribution through CHVs	All residents in 92 lowland and coastal districts sleeping in uncovered spaces and seeking ITNs through a CHV
	Emergency Response	Distribution in response to natural disasters and emergencies	One ITN per two persons in communities most affected by natural disasters, such as cyclones
Social marketing	Keep-Up	Social marketing; commercial sales of subsidized nets	Residents of peri-urban areas who can afford subsidized nets

Note: One additional district was added to the 92 endemic districts for MIP.

Figure 3: Distribution of districts targeted for the 2015 ITN mass distribution campaign

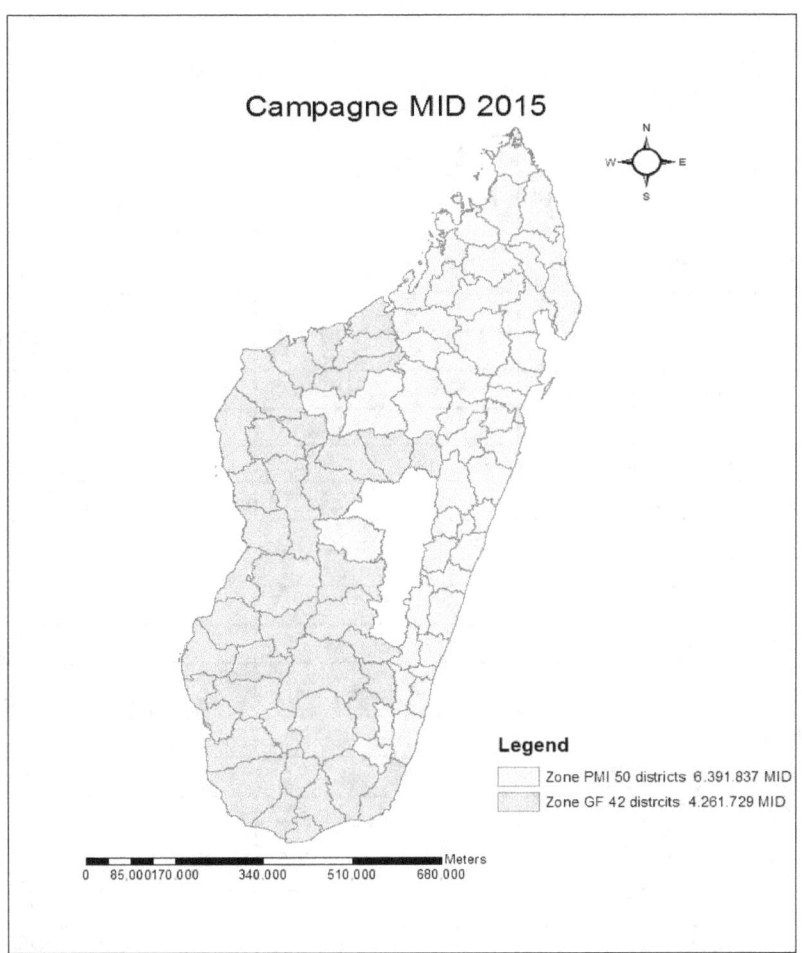

PMI is also supporting the expansion of continuous distribution channels starting with three districts in the South East with high malaria burden. A total of 300,000 ITNs are planned for continuous distribution in 2015. The target population includes pregnant women, vaccinated children, and households with uncovered sleeping spaces such as new couples, immigrants, and households with destroyed ITNs. The approach will rely on CHVs to procure ITNs from supply points and manage the distribution of ITNs to these target populations based on need. Following the lifting of USG restrictions, CHVs will now be able to benefit from close supervision by CSB teams in their communes. PMI is working with RBM partners to scale up continuous distribution to 92 districts with ITNs starting in October 2016, twelve months after the mass distribution campaign. With the Global Fund procured nets, the national program continues to support routine distribution of ITNs to pregnant women and vaccinated children through ANC and EPI clinics at CSB. Performance of this routine distribution continues to be low; according to NMCP data, of the 700,000 nets planned for routine distribution annually, approximately 300,000 are distributed. Following the lifting of USG restrictions, PMI will work to improve this model by incorporating promotion of clinic-based routine distribution into current efforts and reinforce and expand these through integrated ANC. To complement these free distribution channels, PMI continues to support social marketing of highly subsidized ITNs, at a price of approximately \$1.20 per net to the end user. The social marketing approach is focused on peri-urban areas on the East Coast.

Commodity gap analysis

Table 4: ITN Gap Analysis

Calendar Year	2015	2016	2017
Total Targeted Population (92 ITN districts)	19,176,420[1]	19,713,360	20,265,334
Continuous Distribution Needs			
Channel #1: ANC[2]	677,448	754,036	820,746
Channel #2: EPI [3]	578,304	615,057	632,278
Channel #4: CHV continuous distribution[4]	300,000	532,500	3,195,000[5]
Channel #5: Social marketing	150,000	150,000	150,000
Channel #6: Cyclone response & Disaster	50,000	50,000	50,000
Estimated Total Need for Continuous[6]	*1,755,752*	*2,101,593*	*4,848,524*
Mass Distribution Needs			
2015 mass distribution campaign[7]	10,653,567	0	0
Estimated Total Need for Campaigns[8]	*10,653,567*	*0*	*0*
Total Calculated Need: (Routine and Campaign)	**12,409,319**	**2,101,593**	**4,848,524**
Partner Contributions			
ITNs carried over from previous year	1,804,727	0	467,497
ITNs from MoH	0	0	0
ITNs from Global Fund Round NSA2	4,200,000	1,569,090	1,312,960
ITNs planned with PMI funding	4,900,000	1,000,000	1,800,000
Total ITNs Available	**10,904,727**	**2,569,090**	**3,580,457**
Total ITN Surplus (Gap)	**(1,504,592)**	**467,497**	**(1,268,067)[9]**

[1] Estimated population in ITN districts is derived from a 2.8 % annual increase applied to the INSTAT 1993 census population

[2] Needs based on expected 79% ANC coverage in 2015 and projected 5% annual increase in following years

[3] Needs based on expected 80% EPI coverage in 2015

[4] Will resume in October 2016, therefore a small quantity of nets will be distributed to replace about 5% of ITNs distributed during the mass campaign

[5] The need for continuous distribution in 2017 should aim at replacing at least 30% of ITNs distributed during the mass campaign to sustain universal coverage

[6] Nets for Continuous Distribution are estimated needs based ideal situation discussed by RBM

[7] ITN needs for 2015 mass campaign are obtained by dividing the total population in ITN districts by 1.8

[8] No mass distribution is planned in 2016 and 2017

[9] ITN gap will be reduced by Global Fund-procured ITNs (planned for 2015 ANC and EPI distribution), but delayed due to disbursement issues

Plans and justification

FY 2016 funds will be used to support routine and continuous distribution of ITNs in all 92 districts, including districts benefiting from the 2015 September/October ITN mass campaign distribution.

Continuous distribution will start in October 2016, 12 months after the universal mass campaign and will target pregnant women, vaccinated children, and households with uncovered sleeping spaces such as new couples, immigrants, and households with destroyed ITNs. As data from Madagascar continue to show low performance of routine distribution through EPI and ANC, PMI will support the design and implementation of targeted BCC for increased use of malaria prevention measures including ITNs as a priority, especially during pregnancy, and strengthen the routine distribution channels with the re-engagement of PMI support at the health facility level. PMI will continue to monitor ITN durability including physical integrity, survivorship and efficacy of nets distributed in the 2015 mass campaign. Preliminary data from the 2013 net durability assessment is currently being reviewed, and will inform the 2015 monitoring activity.

Proposed activities with FY 2016 funding: ($7,934,000)

1. *Procure ITNs for 2017 distribution:* To procure 1.85 million ITNs for routine distribution via EPI and ANC clinics in 92 districts, and via continuous distribution by CHVs, plus disaster response. Assumes a cost of $3.30/ITN with delivery from port to central warehouse. *($6,120,000)*
2. *Support warehousing and distribution costs in country:* Assumes a cost of $1.00/ITN for logistics from central level to districts, district level warehousing, and transportation to CSBs & CHV sites *($1,700,000)*
3. *Support for continued monitoring of net durability:* Includes monitoring the physical durability of different brands of ITNs that were distributed as part of mass campaigns in 2015. *($100,000)*
4. *Technical assistance of ITN activities:* Support for technical assistance to monitor and evaluate ITN activities. *($14,000)*

2. Indoor residual spraying

NMCP/PMI objectives

The current national strategy, which was recently revised for 2015–2017, recommends IRS in the epidemic-prone CHL, where there is no ITN coverage. The national strategy calls for focalized IRS, based on health facility malaria cases and RDT positivity rates, and epidemic alert reporting. In the most recent IRS round, PMI supported focalized spraying in the CHL and Fringe districts, which was conducted November-December 2014, and a blanket spraying pilot in three high burden districts of the East Coast, which was conducted October–November 2014. Global Fund, in coordination with PMI, has traditionally provided additional support for IRS in the CHL and Fringe districts; however for the past two consecutive years, due to grant disbursement issues and delayed insecticide arrival, the Global Fund was unable to support any spraying.

PMI supports the national IRS strategy and has been prioritizing regions of high malaria burden, such as the East Coast. In 2014, the NMCP agreed that PMI implement a pilot IRS program on the East Coast for two to three years, to see if IRS can impact these areas of higher malaria prevalence. The East Coast was selected by in-country stakeholders due to its high malaria burden, despite universal LLIN coverage. IRS historically has not been used in the East Coast, due to the lack of longer lasting insecticides on the market. The combination of IRS and LLINs is expected to better control malaria in this area of high population density.

In addition to supporting IRS operations, PMI will continue to support routine entomological evaluation of IRS impact and vector-insecticide susceptibility monitoring to inform IRS insecticide class selection.

Progress since PMI was launched

PMI has supported the NMCP's strategy of IRS, as described in the table below. Initially, PMI supported IRS in the lower transmission areas of the Central Highlands, Fringe and Southern districts; however, PMI is now piloting IRS in the higher transmission East Coast districts. With this geographic shift, there has also been a shift in the class of insecticide used for IRS to the longer-lasting organophosphates, due to emerging vector-insecticide resistance and shorter duration of insecticidal effect of other classes. PMI funds have also supported entomological monitoring sites to support the collection of primary entomological indicators across the country. The IRS partnership between the NMCP, PMI, the Global Fund, and the *Institut Pasteur de Madagascar* (IPM), which supports monitoring and evaluation of vector control measures, has also benefitted from coordination and shared expertise.

Table 5: PMI-supported IRS activities (2013-2017)

Calendar Year	Number of Districts Sprayed	Insecticide Used	Structures Sprayed	Coverage Rate	Population Protected
2012/2013	40 communes (CHL+Fringe) Focal IRS	Pyrethroid & Carbamate	87,081	96%	522,292
	7 districts (South)	Organophosphate	284,310	98%	1,259,698
2013/2014	40 communes (CHL+Fringe) Focal IRS	Pyrethroid & Carbamate	82,091	98%	481,301
	7 districts (South)	Organophosphate	261,379	99%	1,106,837
2014	40 communes (CHL+Fringe) Focal IRS	Pyrethroid & Carbamate	125,125	97%	749,965
	3 districts (East)	Organophosphate	149,408	95%	557,419
2015	3 districts (East)	Organophosphate	158,006	-	557,419
	1 district (South East)	Organophosphate	96,980	-	361,736
2016**	3 districts (East)	Organophosphate	158,006	-	573,027
	1 district (South East)	Organophosphate	96,980	-	371,865
2017**	3 districts (East)	Organophosphate	158,006	-	589,072
	1 district (South East)	Organophosphate	96,980	-	382,277

[1] **projected targets = 2.8% annual population increase applied to 2015 targets

Progress during the last 12-18 months

PMI supported blanket IRS in three districts in the East Coast from October–November 2014, and focalized IRS in six districts in the CHL and Fringe from November–December 2014. Organophosphates were used in the East Coast, due to longer residual efficacy, while the CHL and Fringe districts received carbamates or pyrethroid IRS, depending on if they were ITN districts. Additional highlights of the 2014 IRS campaign include:

- A total of 274,533 structures were sprayed (149,408 in the East and 125,125 structures in the CHL) out of 286,928 targeted for spraying, resulting in a 96% spray coverage overall.

- A total of 253,410 of the structures were provided with IEC materials prior to the IRS round.

- There were 3,450 people trained (1,859 in the CHL, and 1,591 in the East), including 1,514 (44%) women.

- Post-spray cone bioassay testing results confirmed 100% mortality (at baseline), indicating high quality spray with the correct dosing of insecticide.

Entomological monitoring: PMI-supported entomological monitoring occurred at ten sites (CHL (4), East (4), and South (2))[14]. Both IRS-targeted and 'similar' comparison sites were included to inform the question of impact and to monitor indicators such as vector-insecticide resistance and IRS residual effectiveness. The three principal malaria vectors *An. gambaie* s.l., *An. funestus,* and *An. mascarensis* were collected and tested. Highlights include: (1) residual insecticidal effectiveness for as long as 10 months post spraying using the long-lasting formulation of organophosphate-class (OP) insecticide, and (2) complete vector-insecticide (OP) susceptibility. While some PMI-supported entomological monitoring sites have evidence of resistance to pyrethroids, the majority of sites indicate susceptibility to carbamate class insecticides.

Plans and justification

With FY 2015 funds, PMI continues to support IRS in the three East Coast districts with organophosphates. PMI is also proposing to add one district in the South East (Farafangana), where epidemiological evidence indicates tramission rates are chronically higher than expected, despite the availability of ITNs. With FY 2016 funds, PMI plans to continue IRS in the East Coast and South East, using organophosphates. Former PMI-supported IRS areas in the CHL will receive PMI support via reinforced surveillance and a reactive case detection OR study (using FY 2015 funds). PMI will also continue to support entomological monitoring in a sample of sites throughout Madagascar, including monitoring of the residual efficacy of insecticide classes, and monitoring in IRS intervention districts, as well as ITN-only districts. Finally, there will also be renewed emphasis on coordination with and capacity building at the NMCP as it implements Global Fund-supported IRS activities in other areas of the country, such as the CHL.

Proposed activities with FY 2016 funding: ($6,848,000)

1. *Conduct IRS*: PMI will support the implementation of IRS using organophosphates in three high burden East Coast districts, plus one additional district in the South East. *($6,611,000)*

2. *Conduct IRS entomology monitoring and evaluation*: Continue to support routine entomological monitoring in 11 sites throughout the country. *($225,000)*

3. *Procure entomological supplies*: Procure entomological supplies to build entomological monitoring capacity in country. *($12,000)*

---

[14] Madagascar 2014 End of Spray Report. PMI / Africa IRS (AIRS) Project (IRS2)

3. Malaria in pregnancy

NMCP/PMI objectives

The NMCP supports a three-pronged approach to MIP including uptake of IPTp with SP, provision and use of ITNs, and prompt diagnosis and treatment of malaria during pregnancy. As part of the national strategy to prevent and limit morbidity associated with malaria during pregnancy since 2004, IPTp is currently implemented in 93 lowland and coastal districts where malaria transmission is stable or seasonal. The decision to implement IPTp in one additional district (Itasy), as compared to the ITN targeted districts was made in 2011 by the RBM stakeholders. The policy excludes the remaining 19 districts in the Central Highlands, which have low prevalence and are epidemic prone. The NMCP supports SP administration to pregnant women at each scheduled ANC visit, with the first dose being administered as early as possible after quickening in the second trimester and subsequent doses of SP provided at least one month apart. With the updating of the IPTp policy in late 2014, PMI and the NMCP are supporting efforts to update routine reporting on frequency of IPTp treatments including IPTp3 and IPTp4. The NMCP recommends that IPTp be administered as directly observed treatment free-of-charge. In addition, iron and folic acid is recommended in the National Protocol for the Fight against Micronutrient Deficiency: 60mg of iron and 400µg of folic acid (low dose) for 180 days (six months) without interruption during pregnancy, to continue after delivery if need be. PMI will work to ensure the NMCP and *Direction de la Santé de l'Enfant, de la Mère et de la Reproduction* (Directorate of Child and Maternal Health and Reproductive Health) are coordinating on the implementation of MIP activities, including IPTp and ITN promotion, and the provision of iron and low dose folate, an essential component of comprehensive ANC services.

Progress since PMI was launched

Overall uptake of IPTp2 has remained constant between two recent MIS surveys (22% in 2011 and 21% in 2013). The 2013–2017 National Strategy objective targets 85% coverage of IPTp2 by 2017 among pregnant women attending ANC. The NMCP revised the monthly HMIS reporting form to capture the number of women who receive two doses of SP for IPTp to monitor progress towards this goal. In November 2014, the NMCP issued a policy directive to reflect the new WHO IPTp recommendations for improved IPTp uptake. With the lifting of USG restrictions, PMI is able to work closely again with the MoH and is providing technical assistance for this national policy change including updating MIP guidelines and ensuring health facility providers are trained in the new policy.

The use of ITNs remains high among pregnant women at 68% in 2013, although this figure represents a decrease from 85% ITN use among pregnant women reported in 2011. The NMCP prioritizes provision of ITNs to pregnant women at their first ANC visit. According to national guidelines, pregnant women who are diagnosed with uncomplicated malaria should receive treatment with quinine in the first trimester and an ACT is recommended for treatment during the second and third trimesters.

The NMCP and Directorate of Child and Maternal Health and Reproductive Health participate on the national ANC working group, which recently proposed the adoption of a new IPTp policy in line with the 2012 WHO IPTp recommendations. To further support MIP interventions, the NMCP has included IPTp as part of integrated ANC services that are promoted during mother and child health promotion weeks in April and October of each year. During these biannual health weeks, vitamin A and deworming medicines are distributed, mass immunization campaigns for children are conducted, ANC sensitization messages are provided to pregnant women, and health promotion messages are disseminated. Program surveillance data show that IPTp uptake peaks during and right after these mother and child health weeks.

Progress during the last 12-18 months

CHVs play an essential role in promoting the use of antenatal services, including encouraging pregnant women to seek IPTp at each ANC visit (after first trimester) and to sleep under an ITN. In FY 2014, PMI funding supported MIP activities through more than 10,343 trained CHVs delivering BCC MIP messages to a third of the country population living in hard to reach places, on the importance of seeking antenatal care (early and frequent visits), taking monthly doses of IPTp, and consistent use of ITNs. In addition, 9,194 PMI-supported CHVs were trained on case management including the importance of referring pregnant women to health facilities for prompt diagnosis and treatment of malaria during pregnancy. PMI-supported CHVs have promoted healthy motherhood through education and community sensitization by promoting ITN use and encouraging pregnant women to seek ANC services. In addition, PMI procured 450,000 treatments of SP in 2014 and an additional 1.8 million SP treatments in 2015 for distribution to approximately 300 NGO and FBO clinics that are currently part of a USAID Maternal Child Health program network.

Despite the high reported rate of ANC attendance (90% of pregnant women attend ANC at least once) and relatively early attendance during the course of the pregnancy (DHS 2008-2009), IPTp uptake remains low. Although the health system experienced SP stockouts for almost two years (due to delays in the Global Fund procurement), it is unclear whether this is the main obstacle to IPTp uptake. Inadequate supervision, lack of refresher training, and staffing shortages have also been reported by partners. Furthermore, some women attend ANC services at private clinics which do not regularly promote IPTp. In response to the reported low uptake of SP for IPTp, the NMCP, with partners, has employed alternative strategies such as using CHVs to deliver targeted messages for the prevention of malaria in pregnancy to pregnant women and encouraging them to attend ANC early and often and to demand IPTp during their visits. CHVs also play an important role in planning, organizing, and conducting health promotion outreach activities, including IPTp for pregnant women, during the biannual mother and child health campaign weeks. With the lifting of restrictions in May 2014, PMI has re-engaged at the health facility level and focused on strengthening MIP activities, including ensuring availability of SP and ITNs. A joint USAID MCH and PMI-supported health facility assessment conducted in the 15 USAID focus regions was undertaken in late 2014 to examine the status and readiness of maternal, newborn and child health services. Preliminary results indicated low capacity of MIP services among the 32 CSBs surveyed: 27% of CSBs administered SP for IPTp and 24% of CSBs had LLINs to distribute to pregnant women at their first ANC visit. Further analysis of MIP services and health provider capacity is pending with submission of the final report.

Commodity gap analysis

Table 6: SP Gap Analysis for Malaria in Pregnancy

Calendar Year	2015	2016	2017
Estimated total population in 93 target districts	19,374,498	19,916,984	20,474,659
Estimated number of pregnant women (4.5%)	871,852	896,264	921,360
SP Needs			
Total number of pregnant women attending ANC *	1,789,040	1,839,134	1,890,628
Total SP Need (in treatments)	**1,789,040**	**1,839,134**	**1,890,628**
Partner Contributions			
SP carried over from previous year	450,000	460,960	27,035
SP from MoH	0	0	0
SP from Global Fund	0	1,405,209	421,706
SP planned with PMI funding	1,800,000	0	500,000
Total SP Available	**2,250,000**	**1,866,169**	**948,741**
Total SP Surplus (Gap)	**460,960**	**27,035**	**(941,887)**

* assumes coverage of ANC 1 at 90%; ANC 2 at 80%; ANC 3 at 60%

% ANC 2 at 50% and ANC 3 at 25%

Plans and justification

With FY 2015 funding, PMI will continue to support progress made at the community level through the CHVs as well as re-launch efforts at the public health facility level to strengthen MIP practices focusing on improving IPTp uptake and ANC attendance. PMI will support training for a national cadre of trainers in MIP and the phased roll out of joint maternal, newborn and child health training for 250 facility-level health providers in five USAID regions in 2015. PMI will also support the NMCP with any revisions needed to malaria and maternal health policy guidelines, aligning them with updated WHO IPTp recommendations and ensuring consistent guidelines between the two national program documents.

With FY 2016 funding, PMI will continue to support strengthening of MIP activities both at the community and public facility levels, including the completion of refresher training for health facility staff in all 93 focus districts. PMI will procure approximately 500,000 treatments of SP for use in 2017, based on the expectation that ANC services uptake would gradually increase following PMI-supported MIP activities at the health facility and the community levels to strengthen and improve IPTp uptake. The NMCP has planned an additional quantity of 421,706 SP treatments through the Global Fund New Funding Model (concept note was submitted in January 2015). Quinine will also be procured through the Global Fund for treatment of malaria during the first trimester of pregnancy. PMI will also continue to support community BCC activities led by the CHVs who encourage pregnant women to attend ANC services and request SP for IPTp, as well as encourage early diagnosis and treatment of malaria in pregnancy with quinine and ACTs.

Proposed activities with FY 2016 funding: ($605,000)

1. Support CHVs with MIP training and implementation: Provide training and implementation support for CHVs in MIP and improve BCC messages and interpersonal communications for MIP. Support includes promoting ITN use, and referrals to health facilities for early and frequent ANC visits, malaria case management, and administration of SP for IPTp at monthly intervals. *($300,000)*

2. Procure SP: PMI will procure approximately 500,000 treatments of SP for IPTp in line with WHO IPTp guidelines for pregnant women attending ANC at health facilities. *($105,000)*

3. Strengthen MIP at public facility level: PMI will support MIP activities at the facility level, including strengthening and improving IPTp uptake, ITN use, and ANC attendance for diagnosis and treatment of malaria during pregnancy. Support includes necessary revisions to update malaria and maternal health program training curriculum and strengthen routine reporting at health facilities on IPTp, train midwife and ANC health facility staff on MIP, and ensure updated MIP policy guidelines are available at facility level for providers. *($200,000)*

4. Case management

a. Diagnosis and Treatment

NMCP/PMI objectives

Under the revised 2013–2017 National Strategic Plan, the goal for case management is to correctly diagnose and treat at least 80% of malaria cases seen at public and private health facilities. Currently RDTs are used at all government primary health care facilities, and at hospital level before confirmation with microscopy. CHVs are also required to use RDTs for diagnosis, and before treatment of malaria at the community level. Madagascar uses combination RDTs (HRP2/pLDH) to detect *falciparum* infections, other infections, and mixed *falciparum*/other infections. A 2007 study showed that, among 709 randomly selected school children seen at eight sites in the country, 5.2% of children were infected with malaria and the prevalence of each *Plasmodium* species was 16.2% *P.falciparum*, 13.0% *P.vivax*, 3.6% *P.ovale*, and 1.8% *P. malariae*[15]. According to the national case management guidelines last updated in April 2013, AS/AQ combination therapy is the first-line antimalarial treatment for

---

[15] Menard et al. Plasmodium vivax clinical malaria is commonly observed in Duffy-negative Malagasy people . PNAS March 2010. (http://www.pnas.org/content/107/13/5967 full.pdf)

uncomplicated malaria in Madagascar, with artemether/lumefantrine (AL) as alternative therapy. For severe malaria, intravenous artesunate is used as first-line treatment, with quinine as second-line treatment. The national guidelines recommend injectable artesunate or quinine, or rectal artesunate for pre-referral treatment of severe malaria for children under five years old at the community and primary health care facilities. In the six pre-elimination districts in the CHL, the national strategy also calls for administration of a single low dose of primaquine in addition to AS/AQ for cases of uncomplicated malaria, except in pregnant women and children less than four years of age. There are currently no guidelines for health facility management of *vivax* malaria due to limited data on safety of primaquine, and limited access to G6PD deficiency testing. PMI will continue to work with the NMCP to ensure that health facility workers and CHVs are well trained to accurately diagnose and manage cases of malaria in health facilities (HF) and at the community level.

Progress since PMI was launched

Diagnostic confirmation using RDTs was introduced by the MoH starting mid-2006 and reached all primary health care facilities by the end of 2008, along with the introduction of ACTs. In 2010, the national iCCM curriculum was revised to include RDT testing of all fever cases among children under five years of age managed by CHVs at the community level. Currently RDTs are used at all government primary health care facilities.

Due to USG restrictions on working with the public health sector, PMI focused exclusively on supporting diagnostics among CHVs and FBO/NGO facilities starting in 2009. PMI procured RDTs for CHVs and FBO/NGO facilities and supported ongoing training, supervision, and use of RDTs by CHVs and private clinics. Most of PMI's case management support was directed at the community level until mid-2014 when restrictions on working with public health facilities were lifted. PMI provided support to two bilateral projects that focus on community delivery of health services that include iCCM of malaria, diarrhea, and pneumonia by CHVs, in line with the MoH policy for community case management by CHVs. Global Fund and UNICEF also provide significant support to the NMCP and the MoH for this approach. These two USAID health bilateral projects cover 15 of the 22 regions in Madagascar, with Global Fund supporting similar activities in the remaining seven regions.

The 2013 MIS survey showed that the proportion of children under five years old with fever who seek advice and treatment has risen from 34% to 44%, and the proportion of children in the same age group who received antimalarial drugs had almost tripled (from 19% to 54%) compared to the 2011 MIS survey. Diagnostic confirmation with RDT and treatment with ACTs is now standard of care, and according to the December 2014 health facility survey, health workers tested 97.4% of patients seen for curative care consultations for whom malaria was suspected; overall adherence to diagnostic guidelines was 93%. Of those patients who tested positive for malaria, all were administered or prescribed an antimalarial (86.1% ACTs) for treatment of uncomplicated malaria.

Progress during the last 12-18 months

With the lifting of restrictions, PMI began a robust plan for re-engaging with the public sector in terms of training, supervision, and other support. The December 2014 PMI-supported health facility survey assessed readiness of HFs to provide high quality care, including the availability of antimalarial drugs recommended by the NMCP, supplies and equipment, trained and supervised health workers, and level of support given to CHVs. In addition, the survey evaluated the appropriateness of health worker practices related to clinical assessment of ill patients, conformity to malaria diagnosis and case management guidelines and data quality. The survey, as summarized in the 'Other relevant evidence on progress' section above, provided valuable baseline information on the current gaps in diagnosis and case management and informed areas for targeted PMI support.

Following the assessment, in February 2015, PMI supported a training of trainers (TOT) activity of 18 clinicians and 16 laboratory technicians from government health facilities who will serve as trainers and supervisors in malaria diagnostics and treatment. These trainers will facilitate cascade training in their respective regions, and conduct supervisory visits at designated health facilities, and establish quality assurance (QA)/quality control (QC) programs within these facilities. The training was conducted in close collaboration with the NMCP who played a major role in the planning and participants' selection.

With FY 2014 funds, PMI supported the training of 9,194 CHVs in malaria diagnostics and treatment. PMI also procured and distributed 802,154 ACTs and 2,780,000 RDTs for CHVs, public health facilities, and FBO/NGO facilities.

Commodity gap analysis

Table 7: RDT Gap Analysis

Calendar Year	2015	2016	2017
RDT Needs			
Target population at risk for malaria[1]	23,670,541	24,333,316	25,014,649
Total number projected fever cases[2]	5,369,103	5,519,438	5,673,982
Percent of fever cases confirmed with microscopy[3]	<1%	<1%	<1%
Percent of fever cases confirmed with RDT[4]	97.4%	97.4%	97.4%
Total RDT Needs	**5,369,103**	**5,519,438**	**5,673,982**
Partner Contributions			
RDTs carried over from previous year	0	0	748,636
RDTs from Global Fund	3,104,175	4,798,074	4,910,418
RDTs planned with PMI funding	2,250,000	1,470,000	0
Total RDTs Available	**5,354,175**	**6,268,074**	**5,659,054**
Total RDT Surplus (Gap)	**(14,928)**	**748,636**	**(14,928)**

[1] Annual population growth rate is 2.8%
[2] Based on population proportion by age group (EDS), fever prevalence (MDG 12/13), number of fever episodes/year (iCCME), and annual growth rate (EDS)
[3] Based on HMIS data
[4] Based on proportion tested when malaria is suspected (2014 Health facility survey)

Table 8: ACT Gap Analysis

Calendar Year	2015	2016	2017
ACT Needs			
Target population at risk for malaria[1]	23,670,541	24,333,316	25,014,649
Total projected number of malaria cases[2]	1,073,821	1,103,887	1,134,796
Total ACT Needs	**1,073,821**	**1,103,887**	**1,134,796**
Partner Contributions			
ACTs carried over from previous year	0	966,468	962,581
ACTs from Global Fund	1,633,776	0	181,043
ACTs planned with PMI funding	406,513	1,100,000	0
Total ACTs Available	**2,040,289**	**2,066,468**	**1,143,624**
Total ACT Surplus (Gap)	**966,468**	**962,581**	**8,828**

[1] Annual population growth rate is 2.8% (DHS)

[2] Malaria cases/ACT need determined by NMCP and based on MIS 2013 parasitemia prevalence and HMIS routine data on RDT positivity rate.

The estimated RDT and ACT needs were calculated during a recent gap analysis exercise using fever prevalence data from the MDG 2012/13 survey, and RDT positivity rate from HMIS routine data, all stratified by age group and population numbers, and taking into account a 2.8% annual growth rate (DHS). Data from health facilities estimate the percentage of severe malaria to be 2% of total malaria cases (22,680 in 2017). We therefore estimate that an average of five vials per treatment is needed for adults and children, and 113,400 vials and ancillary supplies will be purchased through PMI with FY 2016 funds.

Plans and justification

With FY 2015 funds, PMI will support the implementation of outreach diagnostic and case management training and supportive supervision (OTSS) in 40 health facilities from 10 regions during which a cadre of master trainers will be identified and trained. These trainers will implement cascade trainings and play a major role in establishing QA systems in their respective regions. Currently, there is no specific QA system at the central or regional levels although there are adequate facilities, equipment and human resources to implement such activities. Trained laboratory technicians in each region as well as at the central level will be involved in implementation of malaria diagnostic QA systems at the regional and central levels, including malaria diagnostic training, outreach training, slide quality control, and development of manual and laboratory procedures to contribute and maintain their skills.

The iCCM program is being fully integrated into the MoH system, and PMI will continue to provide support through bilateral projects to health facilities and 15,166 CHVs for refresher training, M&E integration and correct use of data monitoring and reporting tools, and routine supervision of CHVs by health staff. Immediately after the lifting of the USG restrictions in May 2014, USAID/Madagascar issued instructions to all USG-funded projects working with the MoH to start planning for re-engagement and direct collaboration with the public health system; specifically supporting CSBs' interaction with CHVs by 1) direct supervision; 2) commodity re-supply; 3) monthly group meetings; and 4) refresher trainings planned and conducted by CSB staff, as needed. Supplies of malaria commodities for CHVs are progressively being transferred to the national supply chain through the districts and primary health facilities. The PMI-supported integrated bilateral projects will work closely with the NMCP to transition responsibilities for supervision and supply provision to health facilities.

With FY 2016 funds, PMI will continue to support both bilateral projects to strengthen malaria case management at both the community level and health facilities in the project areas. Funds will be used to support malaria case management refresher training for staff from all facilities and CHVs in the community, in addition to district health officers. Funds will also be used to build capacity of health facility staff to carry out CHV supervision and to continue to enhance M&E integration and correct use of data monitoring and reporting tools. In addition, PMI will continue to support cascade trainings of laboratory technicians and clinicians in additional regions and districts, and activities related to malaria diagnostic QA/QC systems at the regional and central levels, including laboratory refurbishing. PMI will also procure 113,400 artesunate vials and ancillary supplies for the treatment of severe malaria.

Proposed activities with FY 2016 funding: ($4,510,000)

1. *Procure parenteral artesunate*: Purchase 113,400 artesunate vials and ancillary supplies for treatment of severe malaria at health facilities. *($450,000)*

2. *Procure laboratory consumables and reagents:* PMI will support procurement of laboratory supplies and reagents to support the revitalization of the national reference laboratory. Supplies include 15 microscopes dedicated for regional trainings, spare bulbs, and lens cleaning tissue. This activity is a continuation of supportive supervision activities initiated in FY 2015 to help build capacity at the national reference laboratory, and will be coordinated at the level of the NMCP. *($50,000)*

3. *Refresher training and strengthening of routine supervision and M&E of CHVs and health facilities*: PMI funding will provide support for refresher training in case management and M&E, as well as supportive supervision of CHVs and public and private health facility workers. The NMCP's 2012 treatment guidelines include the use of IV artesunate for the treatment of severe malaria. Therefore, the refresher training will include management of severe malaria. PMI funding will support refresher training for approximately 3,000 CHVs and 3,000 facility-based health workers in the PMI bilateral projects areas (from a total of approximately 2,360 public and private facilities). *($3,600,000)*

4. *Support for national diagnostics quality assurance and quality control.* Building on the findings from the diagnostics assessment conducted in 2014 and the assistance provided to the national laboratory with FY 2015 funds, PMI will continue to enhance and support

national capacity for diagnostics QA/QC. PMI is currently providing technical assistance to the NMCP to finalize the draft QA manual. The implementation of the QA plan will be conducted at the national and regional levels where there are well-trained lab technicians. These technicians will be integrated in all activities related to malaria diagnostic QA systems at the regional and central levels, including malaria diagnostic training, outreach training, slide quality control, and development of manual and laboratory procedures to contribute and maintain their skills. *($400,000)*

5. *Technical assistance to support community case management.* Support for one CDC technical assistance visit to support the case management of malaria. *($10,000)*

b. Pharmaceutical Management

NMCP/PMI objectives

The revised 2013–2017 National Strategic Plan objective is to achieve zero stockouts in public health facilities for ACTs and SP by 2017.

SALAMA, the national central purchasing agency, is responsible for procuring essential medicines and medical consumables for use in the public sector and a portion of the private sector and ensuring their distribution to the district level. All medicines dispensed at public health facilities are sold with a mark-up of approximately 35% of the SALAMA price. Distribution of malaria commodities, like other donated commodities for vertical programs, will not be charged the full 35% rate. Program donated commodities are charged service fees which vary depending on the service or combination of services provided by SALAMA which might include procurement (0.8% service fee), warehousing (1.6% service fee), and/or distribution (2.1% service fee). PMI-procured commodities will be charged fees for distribution in general, and fees for warehousing and distribution if the arrival of commodities at SALAMA does not coincide with immediate distribution plans. With the lifting of the USG restrictions in May 2014, PMI plans to support the revitalization of SALAMA with other USG funding streams, and move to an integrated supply chain system to manage malaria and other USG-funded commodities.

The free distribution of malaria commodities through the public sector has resulted in parallel procurement and distribution channels to the district level. There are also different channels for distributing antimalarial medicines and products within districts, which is based on a push system down to the districts. At the district level, the district pharmaceutical depots are the intermediary points in the public sector supply chain. They are managed primarily by NGOs under a contract with the MoH through the Department of Pharmacies, Laboratories, and Traditional Medicine and they sell to the health facility pharmacies. Free and donated malaria commodities are received and managed by the District Health Office, while the products from SALAMA are managed by the district pharmaceutical depots. In both cases, CSBs are responsible for the collection and transportation of their supplies from the district level to their respective facilities. This limits the quantities that most of them can transport at any one time, as they primarily rely on public transportation. Furthermore, some CSBs are inaccessible for four to six months of the year during the rainy season, thus requiring advanced planning to ensure a reliable supply of health commodities. The absence of a clear distribution schedule leads to frequent stockouts, as indicated in the 2014 PMI-funded health facility assessment. A significant proportion of facilities (between 65.0% and 81.3%) had the various ASAQ treatment courses in stock the day of the survey, but many fewer had a minimum of 20 courses on hand (between 7.7% and 12.1%, depending on weight band). About 42% of facilities had injectable quinine in stock on the day of the survey and about 10% had quinine tablets in stock.

In addition to ACTs, CHVs also dispense other medicines subsidized under a social marketing model financed by USAID. This includes oral rehydration salts plus zinc tablets (approximately $0.22) for the treatment of diarrhea among children under five years of age; cotrimoxazole tablets (approximately $0.09), and cotrimoxazole oral suspension (approximately $0.32) for the treatment of uncomplicated pneumonia. USG-supported CHVs are currently re-supplied through a parallel system, receiving their supplies from private re-supply points run by individuals, often small shops in larger towns and cities. USAID-funded bilateral projects supply these private supply points with commodities. With the lifting of the USG restrictions, the plan is to transition from these private re-supply points, and to have CHVs re-supply their commodities at the CSB. However integration of the CHVs into the CSB system has progressed slowly.

Quality Assurance: The *Agence du Médicament de Madagascar*, which includes the National Medicines Quality Control Laboratory, is responsible for testing most pharmaceutical products destined for use in the country and products already on the market. The medicines quality monitoring program is designed to help the national drug authority to detect substandard and counterfeit medicines and take immediate action to remove such medicines from the market. Prior to the *coup d'état* in 2009, with USG support, the agency established seven peripheral Minilab® testing sites where samples of antimalarials are regularly collected and tested using portable quality testing kits. An additional 15 kits were procured in 2012 with Affordable Medicines Facility – malaria funding, thus fulfilling the goal of expanding drug quality testing sites to the 22 regional reference hospitals in Madagascar. Unfortunately, the Minilab® testing sites are no longer functioning, due to intermittent support for supervision and field activities with the *coup*. PMI plans to support the rebuilding of a QA/QC system, as described in the Diagnosis and Treatment section.

Progress since PMI was launched

PMI has been contributing to the CHV parallel supply chain system by procuring and distributing malaria commodities and by providing technical assistance to support the CHV programs. The CHVs are also trained to provide maternal, newborn, and child health services, including reproductive health counseling, family planning services, nutrition assessments, and treatment for pneumonia and diarrhea.

Progress during the last 12-18 months

PMI and other USAID health funds supported the July 2014 assessment of the national pharmaceutical supply chain which reported the following findings: (1) lack of funding for supply chain logistics at the periphery; (2) multiple vertical program-funded distribution channels lacking integration and coordination; (3) closure of a number of commune and district level drug depots following de-capitalization; (4) recurrent commodity stockouts at health facility level; (5) inexistence of a clear system for moving health commodities from districts to CSB and; (6) low capacity of and inexistence of support mechanisms for human resources in charge of pharmaceutical management. Specific USG-supported interventions are being developed based on the findings of the assessment. The supply chain was designed to move commodities from central to district level, leaving out the logistics for distribution between districts and the peripheral level. Priority will be to reinforce and expand the system to ensure availability of pharmaceutical commodities at commune and community levels.

PMI has supported the MoH to set up the Logistic Committee, which is in charge of strategic planning and the Logistic Management Unit. This committee is composed of representatives from the United Nations Fund for Population, UNICEF, and PMI, and is led by the DPLMT (Direction of Pharmacy). Its role is to coordinate commodity management for different programs. For this aim, specific software, called Pipeline, is implemented for quantification and planning of essential drugs.

PMI continues to support the distribution of ACTs and RDTs via CHVs to the communities located in *fokontany* that are at least five kilometers to the nearest public health facility. As of April 2015, more than 14,000 CHVs were receiving malaria commodities and support from PMI via this parallel supply system. PMI funding procured approximately 2,780,000 RDTs and 881,000 ACTs in 2014 which have been delivered to regional warehouses that supply CHVs in PMI-supported districts. PMI funds have provided assistance to NGO/FBO partners on supply chain management and will also be supporting training on malaria consumption forecasting and commodity ordering in mid-2014.

Plans and justification

PMI and other USG funding streams will continue to support the supply chain and distribution of malaria commodities at both the community level and now at the CSB level. With both USAID and PMI FY 2014 funds, a supply chain intervention is being piloted in 2015 to assess the best way to support supply chain beyond the district level in two regions of Madagascar. Lessons learned from the pilot will be implemented in 2016 onward to strengthen the distribution system. Once a clear plan for the re-integration/consolidation of the CHV supply chain is agreed upon by the stakeholders, some funds will support the integration process, based on the supply chain assessment recommendations. PMI will then work with other stakeholders to phase out the parallel CHV supply chain with FY 2015 funds, and support the national integrated supply chain, where CHVs would resupply at CSBs, using FY 2016 funds.

Proposed activities with FY 2016 funding: ($1,200,000)

1. *Warehouse and LMIS optimization:* PMI will support the revitalization of the national supply chain system with a warehouse and logistics management information system (LMIS) optimization. This activity will build off of the supply chain assessment recommendations, and work to ensure functionality of the national and regional warehouses. This activity will be co-funded with other USAID Health Office programs. *($400,000)*

2. *Strengthen the supply chain for malaria commodities:* PMI will ensure the continuous supply of RDTs and ACTs via an integrated national supply chain system. This activity includes training of MoH staff at the district and lower levels on the implementation of the revitalized supply chain system. This system will integrate the parallel CHV supply chain system, and activities will include integrated quantification and forecasting,

curriculum development, and supervision support. This activity will be co-funded with other USAID Health Office programs. *($800,000)*

5. Health system strengthening and capacity building

PMI supports a broad array of health system strengthening activities which cut across intervention areas, such as training of health workers, supply chain management and health information systems strengthening, drug quality monitoring, and NCMP capacity building.

NMCP/PMI objectives

The NMCP leads national control efforts through the formulation of policies and strategies, coordination of all partners involved in malaria control, and implementation, as secondary recipients, of most of the Global Fund malaria grants. The NMCP coordinates the RBM partnership comprising several partners including PMI, UNICEF, WHO, private sector companies, local and international NGOs, research institutions, and other government services, in an effort to optimize efforts and investments in the fight against malaria in Madagascar. However, challenges for the NMCP include ensuring effective coordination from the central level down to the district level with other government directorates who have equal responsibility in disease control, epidemiological surveillance, program oversight and reporting, and training and supervision of staff who lack skills in malaria control. The directorates in charge of health districts, maternal and child health, and epidemiological surveillance are the ones who must coordinate most closely with the NMCP.

Progress since PMI was launched

Following five years of political crisis and a staff hiring freeze since 2009, the MoH is currently facing a critical staff shortage at all levels of the public health system, especially for service provision below the national level. In addition, health workers are not distributed evenly throughout the country. More than 65% of the population lives beyond five kilometers of a health facility, frequently in inaccessible places. Along with Global Fund and UNICEF, PMI helped train a cadre of community health workers, in the ratio of two per *fokontany*. The CHVs provide preventive services and treat uncomplicated cases of the three most common childhood illnesses: pneumonia, diarrhea, and malaria. CHVs refer severe cases to the nearest primary health facility. The shortage of staff, both in terms of their numbers and level of training, affects the quality of service at each level of the service delivery pyramid.

Public and non-governmental sector capacity to plan effectively and manage health programs is weak, particularly in the areas of financial and administrative management, and the collection and use of data for program planning and monitoring. National health infrastructure, information and commodity management and logistics systems are extremely weak, and much remains to be done at central, regional, and district levels to ensure sustainable health financing.

Progress during the last 12-18 months

With the official lifting of the USG restrictions in May 2014, PMI is working with USAID Madagascar to strengthen specific health systems areas, starting with supply chain, HMIS, in-service training and supervision, and leadership/management and governance strengthening. PMI funds contributed to a USG assessment of the pharmaceutical supply chain in July/August 2014.

As a result, support to SALAMA, the national parastatal in charge of supply chain, is underway. This support includes training, facilitating needed restructuring, and piloting a new distribution scheme which runs from the central to the commune level. A preliminary assessment of the HMIS was completed in April 2015, and a subsequent in-depth evaluation of data collection and management, and plans to reinforce HMIS capacity are underway, with the aim of installing DHIS2 (an integrated web-based data management system) from the national level down to the district by 2016. In addition to the two major assessments during the last quarter of 2014, PMI supported a health facility assessment and a malaria BCC determinants study to inform malaria programming, including the design of the FY 2016 MOP. Along with other USAID health funding, PMI contributed to the assessment of maternal and child health services which included findings on quality of IPTp services in health facilities.

Plans and justification

PMI will focus on building NMCP technical and managerial capacity at all levels of the health care system, both through implementing partners and direct support to the NMCP and other government partners. PMI will work with the NMCP, Global Fund, and RBM partners to support the implementation of the national strategy and national malaria monitoring and evaluation plan, as discussed in the November 2014 midterm review. PMI will support improvement of quality services through on-the job training coupled with increased frequency of supervisory visits.

Regarding monitoring and evaluation, PMI will support refresher training, reinforcement of the analytical capacity at the central and district levels, and support for the development of a system to promote the centralization and storage of data (including surveys and program reports) gathered by various NGOs, implementing partners, and other donors. (Costs referenced in Monitoring and Evaluation section).

With regards to malaria BCC activities, PMI will continue to work with stakeholders to periodically review, update, and harmonize malaria behavior change communication messages. PMI will also support capacity strengthening of the NMCP communication team. (Costs referenced in BCC section).

To help the NMCP reach preventive and curative coverage targets for key malaria interventions, PMI will continue collaboration with other partners to support the NMCP, specifically to increase capacity at all levels to plan, implement, supervise, forecast commodity needs; improve distribution systems; coordinate with partners; and monitor and evaluate malaria activities. PMI staff and implementing partners will continue to provide on-the-job training and support to improve NMCP management and coordination capacity. With the complexity of malaria stratification in Madagascar, the NMCP must acquire adequate managerial and technical capacity to provide effective leadership and coordination within the MoH from the central level down to the district level, with other Government ministries, with partners, and with different communities. (Costs referenced in other MOP sections)

In addition, PMI will work to strengthen NMCP training and supportive supervision capacity of malaria case management and diagnostics at central, regional, and districts level (costs referenced in Case Management section). Of particular attention, PMI will support the strengthening of the MoH pharmaceutical and commodity management system, including support to SALAMA's capacity to store, distribute, and forecast commodity needs. (Costs referenced in Pharmaceutical and Commodity Management section).

Proposed activities with FY 2016 funding: ($258,000)

1. *Strengthen NMCP leadership, management, and governance*: PMI will continue to build the national capacity for leadership, management and governance, in conjunction with other USG funding streams, through on-the-job training. *($200,000)*

2. *Support for Malaria Peace Corps Volunteers*: PMI will continue to support three PCVs nested with implementing partners to support malaria control interventions. In addition, FY 2016 funds will support one Malaria Volunteer based in the capital, to coordinate all malaria activities with other PCVs. Funding also includes support for Small Projects Assistance (SPA) programs by Peace Corps. *($58,000)*

Table 9: Health Systems Strengthening Activities

HSS Building Block	Technical Area	Description of Activity
Health Services	Case Management	PMI will improve, through training and supportive supervision, QA/QC systems to monitor laboratory diagnostic services quality
Leadership, Management &Governance	Health Systems Strengthening	PMI will build NMCP technical and managerial capacity at all levels, both through implementing partners and direct support to the NMCP to increase effectiveness
Health Workforce	Health Systems Strengthening	PMI will support the strengthening of MoH pharmaceutical and commodity management system, including support for SALAMA's capacity to store, distribute & forecast commodity needs
Health Information	Monitoring and Evaluation	PMI will strengthen routine health data & disease surveillance system, planning, forecasting and program management, through health staff M&E training and the support of a web-based system for data.
Essential Medical Products, Vaccines, and Technologies	Case Management	PMI will support improved forecasting, procurement, quality control, storage and distribution of malaria commodities (insecticide-treated nets, artemisinin-based combination therapies and rapid diagnostic tests)

6. Behavior change communication

NMCP/PMI objectives

The NMCP strategic plan supports BCC as an essential component of its malaria prevention and control interventions and established a BCC working group which supports major communication events such as World Malaria Day and mass ITN distribution campaigns. The NMCP developed a five-year BCC action plan (2013-2017) with the overall objective of achieving 85% use of malaria prevention and case management services among the target population. Specific objectives include: strengthening adoption of favorable behaviors in malaria control among individuals and communities; and encouraging involvement of stakeholders and actors from different sectors in malaria control efforts. To achieve these objectives, the BCC plan calls for strengthening advocacy, BCC and social mobilization activities, reinforcing capacities of all stakeholders involved in malaria control through periodic training, and active participation of the community through CHVs, health providers, community leaders, and religious groups. The Global Fund and PMI are the main donors supporting the NMCP's BCC activities.

Progress since PMI was launched

At community level, each village or *fokontany* has identified two CHVs, one focusing on child health and one responsible for maternal and reproductive health. A total of approximately 34,000 CHVs exist nationwide to provide BCC messages and assist in community mobilization; however not all CHVs are currently active or supported by partners. PMI supports over 14,000 CHVs in 80 districts implementing integrated community management of childhood illness activities including diagnosis and treatment of malaria, as well as providing interpersonal malaria BCC messages to promote correct care seeking and prevention behaviors. With FY 2013 funding, PMI supported implementing partners to update BCC training materials for use by CHVs, including ensuring IPTp and ITNs were addressed. Between October 2013 and March 2014, more than 5,000 PMI-supported CHVs participated in behavioral change empowerment training, which focused on promoting and educating pregnant women as well as men on ANC, ITNs, iron and folate, and IPTp with SP. During this same period, PMI-supported CHVs reached over 1.8 million people (59% were women) through home visits, group education sessions and mass media events in the targeted project areas.

PMI supports an integrated "healthy family" behavior change communication (BCC) campaign focused on increasing knowledge and adoption of preventive behaviors and utilization of malaria commodities for prevention and appropriate treatment. The "healthy family" campaign is broadcast twice weekly by two radio stations with national reach, including the national radio. Before being aired, the malaria prevention messages, along with other maternal and child health desired behaviors, are designed and tested to accommodate accepted local language and culture.

PMI also supports a third-year malaria Peace Corps Volunteer to serve as a focal point and coordinate with other PCVs in Madagascar on malaria BCC efforts and overall health system strengthening. PCVs have promoted malaria BCC messages through their community development activities, participated in World Malaria Day, and highlighted BCC messages at soccer events to raise awareness about malaria control.

The most recent KAP survey conducted in September of 2014 showed that over half (56.6%) of the respondents said they had heard or seen at least one message about malaria prevention or treatment during the last year. The messages most commonly heard or seen were about ITNs (40.0%), MIP (39.4%), the severity of malaria (11.2%) and the risk of contracting malaria (10.6%). The majority (82.7%) of the respondents also knew that mosquito bites cause malaria, and more than two thirds (71.7%) of the respondents mentioned two or more symptoms. About four fifths (86.8%) of the respondents named one or more correct ways to prevent malaria while about a fifth (19.5%) mentioned one or more incorrect preventive methods. About 64.2% of the respondents agreed that people only get malaria when there are lots of mosquitoes around and

58.0% agreed that their children were so healthy that they could recover quickly if they had malaria. In addition, 94.4% of the survey respondents said that each case of malaria could potentially lead to death and 88.4% said they almost always worried that their child might have malaria when they had a fever. Almost two thirds (62.1%) of respondents were aware of a place in their community where they could purchase bed nets. The majority (95.8%) of the respondents believed that sleeping under a bed net every night was the best way to avoid malaria. Nonetheless, about half (49.3%) said that many people sleeping under a mosquito net still got malaria. Few (9.2%) caretakers knew that SP was the prophylaxis given to pregnant women to prevent malaria, and women (11.1%) were considerably more likely than men (3.8%) to mention SP for the prevention of malaria in pregnant women. Awareness about ACT was not very common: about a quarter (23.8%) of the respondents mentioned ACT as a medication for treating malaria and almost half of respondents (46.7%) did not know what drug was used to treat malaria.

These findings clearly show the need to invest in more targeted BCC to increase knowledge and awareness about malaria interventions, improve IPTp uptake, and promote prompt and appropriate care-seeking for treatment of malaria.

Progress during the last 12-18 months

PMI has been instrumental in reinvigorating the in-country BCC Technical Working Group which includes BCC specialists of PMI implementing partners and NMCP and MoH counterparts. This now well-functioning group reviews key malaria messages and harmonizes them among members. There is significant representation in the group in terms of geographical coverage as well. Because of causal linkages between natural disaster and malaria outbreaks, this working group is also collaborating with BCC colleagues with the National Office of Disaster Management within Ministry of the Interior.

Preliminary results of the 2014 KAP survey found that the PMI BCC program may benefit from further investments in aligning risk perception with the realities on malaria in Madagascar, especially in areas of unstable transmission where malaria epidemics occur at irregular intervals. More understanding is needed, particularly among caregivers, regarding the severity of infection and their susceptibility. The study also found that in the Sub-desert South and Central Highland zones, interpersonal communication about key prevention and treatment behaviors could also be beneficial.

Plans and justification

Based on progress and output from the in-country BCC working group, recent studies, and field visits, the NMCP is committed to implementing more efficient BCC tools and approaches based on studies, lessons learned, and site visit findings.

Because of regional differences in culture and normative behaviors, a Global Fund-supported anthropological study will take place in 2016 to further refine BCC campaigns and activities beyond the findings of the BCC assessment. Presently, on the Eastern and Western coasts, BCC messages for malaria control are disseminated all year round, because transmission is perennial. In the Central Highlands, Fringe and the South, BCC activities are intensified during the peak transmission season. Following the Global Fund-supported study, a more refined approach will inform the NMCP and malaria partners about any regional differences in community behaviors, low results from a strategy (e.g. low use of IPTp, outbreak despite ITN campaign) and cultural practices and guide the development and adaption of targeted malaria BCC messages for different malaria transmission zones, if appropriate.

Targeted BCC activities will include promoting the use of ITNs by the general population and by pregnant women and children under five years of age in particular, promoting community acceptance of IRS, early and regular antenatal clinic attendance to ensure uptake of IPTp, and prompt diagnosis and treatment of malaria.

To complement mass media efforts, PMI will continue to support interpersonal communication and community-based behavior change interventions implemented through re-engagement with the public sector as well as through NGOs and CHVs. The CHVs will provide outreach to families to convey malaria prevention awareness messages and to teach personal preventive behaviors through participatory radio listening groups, small group education sessions, and home puppets, which are popular in Madagascar. Skits and dramas will also be used to convey messages and promote behaviors. Use of interpersonal communication approaches will be prioritized over the use of mass media, with the aim of approximately 70% of BCC funding going towards interpersonal communication in communities where awareness of malaria is high enough for this approach to be effective.

Proposed activities with FY 2016 funding: ($1,405,000)

1. *Support for malaria BCC activities at the community and health facility level*: Support the implementation of harmonized malaria messages at the community and health facility level using the two bilateral projects in Madagascar. PMI will support malaria messages reaching rural areas through community-based interpersonal communication by CHVs, skits and dramas, mobile video unit shows, and radio spots. Targeted and general BCC activities will be implemented to mobilize traditional and religious community leaders and civic organizations to promote malaria prevention and control. Madagascar has strong traditional structures in place at the community level and more than 18 ethnic groups in country. PMI will need to work closely with stakeholders and partners to engage these groups in malaria control. PMI will reengage health care providers at the facility level to ensure they have access to and utilize BCC materials and tools available through malaria partners and help develop key malaria messages that are standardized and harmonized across all malaria partner activities. Investments will be made across all intervention areas including ITNs, IRS, malaria in pregnancy, and case management with tailored messages and approaches as informed by the 2014 KAP survey, and the FY 2015 funded anthropological survey on the use of ITNs.

   a. ITNs: Using interpersonal communication with CHVs, activities will focus on increasing ITN use among those who have access to a net by addressing relevant ideational elements and improving understanding of how durable nets are and how to best maintain them to maximize their durability and effectiveness. Net promotion programs will provide forums for discussions about nets in addition to mid-media channels such as radio. Household decision-makers, particularly men, will be encouraged to be involved in the allocation of nets within the household to ensure equitable distribution of nets for all sleeping spaces. Misuse of LLINs will also be discouraged.

b. IRS: Strategic health communication programs will aim to reinforce community acceptance for IRS while addressing negative attitudes that could complicate the implementation of IRS campaigns.

c. Malaria in pregnancy: BCC programs will aim to champion the effectiveness of IPTp to prevent malaria through strategically designed messages that capitalize on the high prevalence of ANC care to develop a norm that establishes taking SP as a critical part of antenatal care. In addition to advocacy to ensure continuous availability of SP in health facilities, efforts to improve interpersonal communication and technical skills of health providers with respect to IPTp will be undertaken. These activities will be particularly important in the Sub-desert transmission zone, where IPTp-related ideation was particularly poor. Special outreach will be made to women who are not married as they are less likely to adhere to the recommended IPTp treatment than married women.

d. Case management: A focus of case management BCC activities at the health facility level will aim to reinforce confidence in malaria diagnostics and discourage the use of ACTs with a negative RDT result. These strategies will be integrated into interventions aimed at improving health care providers' competence to manage fever and malaria. Programs will seek to increase knowledge of ACTs in areas of unstable transmission at the community level and increase caregiver confidence in their ability to seek diagnosis and treatment of malaria in areas of stable transmission through IPC with CHVs. Forums that are inclusive of women are particularly salient to this context as they are marginalized in decisions regarding child health. *($ 455,000)*

2. *Implementation of malaria BCC activities at the national level:* Support the reproduction of the malaria toolkit and support materials, and the implementation of mass media activities. Communication through mass media will use integrated malaria messaging including the four key messages related to correct use of ITNs, acceptance of IRS where applicable, preventing malaria among pregnant women, including promoting uptake of IPTp and early and prompt care seeking for malaria case management. Special efforts will be deployed for the uptake of IPTp and appropriate care seeking. PMI will also support coordination of BCC messages at the national level that will include updating the standard and harmonized package of essential BCC malaria messages based on feedback from FY 2015 implementation of this activity. *($950,000)*

7. Monitoring and evaluation

NMCP/PMI objectives

The objectives of the revised 2013–2017 National Strategy for Epidemic Surveillance and Response are primarily to strengthen the M&E system in order to detect and control most epidemics, and to assure that at least 80% of malaria data are reported from health facilities. Following a midterm review of the Strategic Plan and using recent malaria data, the country was stratified into two operational zones based on malaria epidemiology: 1) an endemic zone or high transmission area that includes the East Coast and the West Coast; and 2) a non-endemic or low transmission area covering the Central Highlands and the Sub-arid South. This reclassification is a move away from the previously identified three operational zones: control, consolidation, and pre-elimination zones. Efforts to establish pre-elimination zones continue; the NMCP is currently working with partners to establish measures to declare a pre-elimination zone covering six districts in the CHL with <2% parasitemia rate among children under five, and less than 5% microscopy and RDT positivity.

Progress since PMI was launched

The current M&E system for malaria is comprised of: 1) the national HMIS, which reports malaria cases and deaths monthly from health facilities; 2) the Integrated Disease Surveillance and Response system, which is based on a weekly reporting of notifiable diseases; 3) an integrated fever sentinel surveillance system, which provides highly accurate and rapid reporting of data from 34 individual sentinel health facilities and 73 CHVs; and 4) population-based surveys such as DHS and MIS. Additional M&E data are available, including insecticide resistance monitoring, therapeutic efficacy studies conducted approximately every two years, and pharmacovigilance monitoring.

The national HMIS system is the MoH's integrated monthly routine reporting system that relies on paper-based reporting from health facilities (and to a limited extent from communities) to the district level, and from the district level to the national level via electronic database transfer. The HMIS actually consists of multiple databases for various reporting sectors: primary health facility data (GeSIS), community health, human resources in health facilities, and commodities. The MoH developed an HMIS strengthening strategy in 2013 and recently made some progress in harmonizing indicators across programs, revising health facility registers, and updating GeSIS in December 2014. Compilation of malaria data reported through GeSIS is completed with the assistance of a data manager supported by Global Fund grants. Starting in 2008, reports have been entered into the central database and are available for use by the NMCP. The NMCP has also created a website for sharing program information: http://www.pnlp-madagascar.mg.

The Integrated Disease Surveillance and Response system (IDSR), implemented jointly by the MoH division responsible for epidemic surveillance (DVSSE) and WHO, is based on a weekly paper-based and SMS aggregate reporting of suspect and confirmed cases on the list of notifiable conditions that includes malaria. The IDSR, in theory, is a surveillance system covering all health facilities in the country and allowing early detection and investigation of outbreaks. Since the beginning of its implementation in Madagascar in 2000, however, its funding has been limited and unstable, leading to uneven implementation. For this reason, the IDSR is functional only in 18 districts out of 112 in the country, and completeness and timeliness of data reporting have been very poor. Other major limitations of this system are its inability to efficiently share data across health programs, and very limited data quality control and supportive supervision.

PMI has been supporting a fever surveillance system managed by a bilateral project at 34 sentinel sites that also provides weekly data on fever causes. This system uses syndromic surveillance coupled with confirmation by diagnostic testing to systematically classify all fever cases as a laboratory-confirmed malaria case, a suspected case of an outbreak-prone disease (i.e., arbovirus, influenza, malaria, plague), or other fevers. Aggregate data on the number of fever cases is transmitted daily to the central level from each site using short message service phone technology, including demographic information, clinical symptoms, RDT results, and history of antimalarial treatment before clinical consultation. Weekly feedback on reported data is provided to the fever sentinel sites, and a quarterly newsletter summarizing the reported cases and trends is distributed to the RBM partners and other stakeholders. The fever sentinel sites system is currently the only readily available source of timely malaria morbidity trend data available to PMI and the USG, and it was responsible for the detection and response to potential epidemics in several regions of Madagascar in 2012 and 2013, and most recently in December 2014 and January 2015. This system will soon be complemented by the Malaria Early Warning System (MEWS) framework, which will include analysis of climate data, and program interventions for predicting epidemics.

The baseline national household survey used for tracking malaria indicators is the 2008-2009 DHS. Follow-up national surveys include the 2011 and 2013 MIS. Additionally, a large household survey to measure progress toward the MDGs in Madagascar was funded by United Nations partners and health donor partners, including PMI. The MDG survey was completed in January 2013 and replaces the 2013–14 DHS survey. This household survey used a combination of two large standard household survey questionnaires: the DHS questionnaire and Living Standards Measurement Survey questionnaire. The survey estimated child mortality at 62 per 1,000 live births, which represents a small decrease from 2009. The maternal mortality rate stagnated and remained high at 479 deaths per 100,000 live births, down from 498 deaths per 100,000 live births according to the 2009 DHS.

PMI and the Global Fund have been supporting first-line antimalarial drug (AS/AQ) efficacy monitoring every two years. The 2009 study conducted in Maevatanana showed 100% efficacy of AS/AQ, and subsequent studies at two sites in 2010, Vatomandry and Miandriavazo, showed 98.8-100% efficacy. In 2012/13 therapeutic efficacy (TES) studies funded by GF in four sites representing different transmission areas showed 98-100% efficacy. The latest PMI funded TES studies in three fever surveillance sites in 2014 showed 95-100% efficacy of AS/AQ.

Progress during the last 12-18 months

The 2013 MIS, co-funded by PMI, has provided the second nationwide report of parasitemia results in Madagascar. Data shows that only two of the five malaria operational zones, the East coast and Central Highlands had a decrease in parasitemia prevalence in children under five compared to MIS 2011. The other transmission areas showed increases in parasitemia prevalence. This can be partially explained by the timing of the implementation of both surveys in relation to ITN mass campaigns. MIS 2011 was conducted in April-May 2011 and after completion of the rolling ITN mass campaign in all 92 districts in 2009/10. In 2013, however, the MIS survey was conducted when only East Coast districts had been covered by the 2012 ITN mass campaign, while other malaria transmission zones had not benefitted yet from the rolling campaign completed in late 2013. These results help confirm data from previous surveys and studies, showing that access to ITNs is closely linked with parasitemia prevalence; with increased ITN access, parasitemia prevalence decreases, but with reduced access the opposite occurs. A summary of the parasitemia data is shown in figure 4.

Figure 4: Parasitemia prevalence

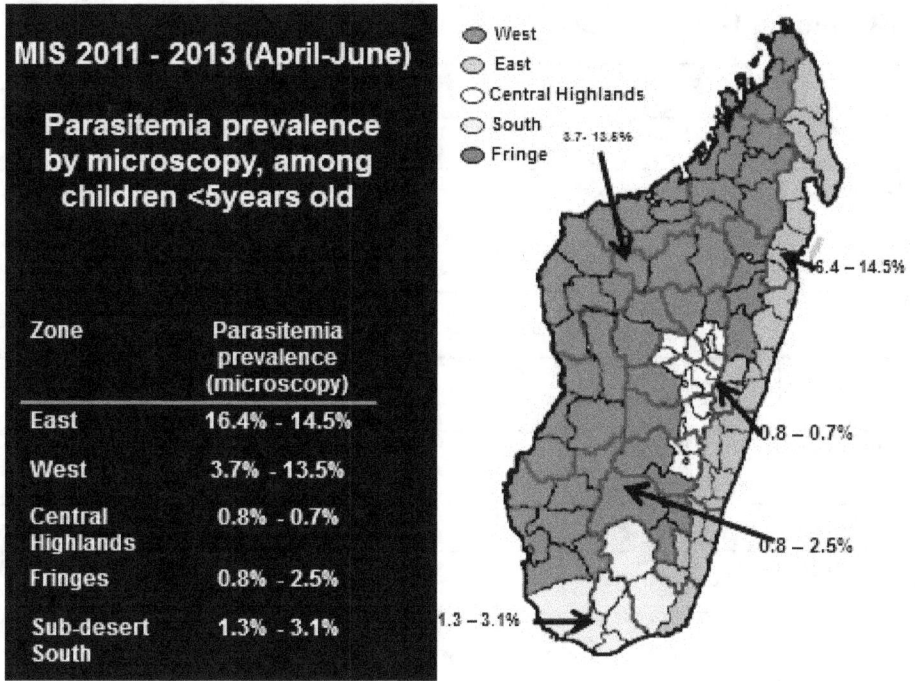

Zone	Parasitemia prevalence (microscopy)
East	16.4% - 14.5%
West	3.7% - 13.5%
Central Highlands	0.8% - 0.7%
Fringes	0.8% - 2.5%
Sub-desert South	1.3% - 3.1%

Earlier this year, PMI supported a preliminary assessment of the national HMIS system and the country's various disease surveillance systems, including the fever sentinel sites, and the IDSR. The main findings included a fragmented HMIS system with duplication of data collection, and a poorly functioning disease surveillance system with low coverage. In light of these findings, technical support to the MoH will start this year with a comprehensive assessment of the HMIS and disease surveillance systems. The objective is to conduct a detailed data quality review, including: 1) a thorough review of the data collection process, organizational structure, and challenges; 2) a review of the different databases to assess quality of data reporting; and 3) an assessment of the performance in providing quality malaria surveillance data. The results of the assessment will allow the country to develop an action plan prioritizing system strengthening activities for a national HMIS system designed to ensure that high-quality program data are available and accessible, in near real time, for use by health programs, including malaria, at both the district and national levels. Additionally, the plan will propose one integrated disease surveillance system including the fever sentinel sites and the IDSR that will cover all regions of the country to accurately and rapidly produce data to help detect malaria and epidemic-prone diseases. PMI and other stakeholders will support the MoH in these capacity strengthening activities, and will transition the management of the fever surveillance sites from the bilateral project to the MoH once capacity is established.

Table 10. Monitoring and Evaluation Data Sources

Data Source	Survey Activities	Year								
		2010	2011	2012	2013	2014	2015	2016	2017	2018
National-level Household surveys	Demographic Health Survey (DHS)									X
	MDG Survey				X					
	Malaria Indicator Survey (MIS)		X		X			X		
	National Population Census							X	X	
Health Facility and Other Surveys	School-based malaria survey					X				
	Health facility survey					X				
	Health facility survey (MIP)					X				
Malaria Surveillance and Routine System Support	Support to malaria surveillance system through IDSR	X	X	X	X	X	X	X	X	X
	Support to parallel routine malaria info system (GF) *	X	X	X	X	X	X			
	Support to HMIS					X	X	X	X	X
Therapeutic Efficacy	In vivo efficacy testing			X		X		X		X
Entomology	Entomological surveillance and resistance monitoring	X	X	X	X	X	X	X	X	X
Other malaria-related evaluations	KAP survey					X				
	Anthropological survey							X		
Other Data Sources	Malaria Impact Evaluation							X		

* Not PMI-funded

Plans and justification

PMI will continue to support fever sentinel sites in FY 2016, along with a MIS, a therapeutic efficacy study, and HMIS and disease surveillance strengthening activities.

With FY 2016 funding, PMI will continue to support malaria surveillance and survey activities. This includes continued support to 15 of the 34 fever sentinel sites (FSS) collecting weekly data on fever and malaria to monitor the impact of program interventions. This support will be transitioned to MoH once national capacity is strengthened. More specifically, following the re-engagement with the GOM in May 2014, PMI planned activities to build the capacity of the NMCP in malaria surveillance through technical assistance from *Institut Pasteur de Madagascar* with FY 2015 resources. Beginning in 2016, there will be a progressive transfer of fever sentinel sites management to the NMCP. Support for community and health facility-based surveillance and routine epidemic surveillance will also be provided to the MoH through the strengthening of IDSR. PMI will support health staff trainings and supervisory visits, strengthening data monitoring and analysis at the central and district levels, and support to promote the centralization and storage of data gathered by various implementing partners.

PMI will continue to help strengthen the national HMIS system through targeted support to the NMCP and MoH for training, supportive supervision and materials for CHVs and health facility staff, and the establishment of a data warehouse at the national level on a web-based District Health Information System Version 2 (DHIS2) platform.

An impact evaluation is also being planned to measure the impact of malaria control interventions such as ITNs, IRS, and malaria case management with ACTs. Data from national surveys and routine systems will be used for this activity.

Proposed activities with FY 2016 funding: ($ 1,360,000)

1. *Continued support for 15 of the 34 fever sentinel sites:* to monitor trends in malaria morbidity and mortality in different transmission areas, and help predict epidemics. These sentinel sites include primary health facilities, hospitals and CHVs. Disease surveillance capacity will be progressively transferred to the MoH, including the integration of this platform into the national surveillance system. *($300,000)*

2. *Support for HMIS system strengthening:* through targeted support to the NMCP and the MoH for training, supportive supervision and materials for CHVs and health workers, and a national data warehouse on a web-based platform. This HMIS strengthening activity will build off activities initiated in 2015, and includes the PMI-supported design and implementation of a PRISM assessment to measure the system performance, establish a baseline, and identify factors to influence performance. The subsequent recommendations will lead to a work plan with appropriate and contextualized interventions including training, supervision, materials, and the establishment of a data warehouse on a DHIS2 platform interlinking up to five databases. This multi-year activity is supported by other donors, including the Global Fund. Although the national strategy is supporting the expansion of SMS for epidemic surveillance, PMI will focus more on technical assistance with the bilateral project to build the capacity through training and technology transfer. *($700,000)*

3. *Strengthen national disease surveillance system:* to continue implementation of community and health facility based surveillance activities, provide targeted support to MoH and NMCP for surveillance, and epidemic detection, and establish an integrated disease surveillance system. The project will provide technical assistance to the MoH by conducting training and assisting the MoH in building a SMS-based system to strengthen and expand the IDSR data collection and management system. The long term plans are to build capacity of the IDSR system that will serve as the primary disease surveillance system, including malaria, and for the fever sentinel sites to be integrated into the system. *($250,000)*

4. *Support the Impact Evaluation:* Provide operational support for Madagascar's Impact Evaluation of malaria control interventions using existing data from national surveys. *($100,000)*

5. *Technical assistance:* One CDC TDY for the support of PMI Madagascar M&E activities, including support for the impact evaluation. The USAID TDY will be centrally funded. *($10,000)*

8. Operational research

<u>NMCP/PMI objectives</u>

The NMCP Operational Research objectives were revised during the November 2014 midterm review of the 2013–2017 national malaria strategy. Priority areas are: (1) the use of sterile mosquitoes for malaria control; (2) therapeutic efficacy studies, and; (3) anthropological studies to inform behavior change communication activities, in association with malaria burden and access to services.

<u>*Progress during the past 12-18 months*</u>

The Central Highlands of Madagascar have very low malaria transmission and the area has a long history of receiving IRS in the 1990s and 2000s. With funding from PMI and Global Fund, the CHL received four years of blanket spraying (all communes in the supported districts) from 2008 to 2012 and transitioned to focalized spraying, targeting the communes in selected districts with the highest malaria incidence, in 2013, according to the national strategic plan. Communes have been targeted for spraying by calculating estimated malaria incidence from health facility data. However, concerns about the completeness and accuracy of health facility data are compounded by low rates of care-seeking in the formal sector in Madagascar, and have raised questions about the validity of the current approach to estimating transmission intensity and prioritizing communes for IRS. As a method to validate facility-based data, as well as other approaches (e.g., school absenteeism data) for prioritizing malaria interventions, a school-based malaria serology survey was conducted as a gold standard for prioritizing communes for focalized IRS. Preliminary data analysis showed that health facility data identified 21 of 30 communes with the highest transmission determined by serology, for a sensitivity of 70%. This study showed that routine data performed relatively well but did not identify all malaria hotspots. A draft manuscript describing the findings from this study is being prepared.

To help the NMCP determine the most effective approaches to further reduce and maintain malaria transmission at low levels, PMI is supporting operational research on the effectiveness of malaria reactive case detection with FY 2014 and FY 2015 funds. The study will examine reactive case detection around passively detected malaria cases, in order to help the NMCP determine the most feasible and effective approaches to further reduce and maintain malaria transmission at low levels. Funds will also include support to one Peace Corps Volunteer who will provide dedicated support to the reactive case detection pilot in the CHL.

Table 11: PMI-funded Operational Research Studies

Completed OR Studies			
Title	**Start Date (est.)**	**End Date (est.)**	**Budget**
Use of serology to validate health facility-based data for prioritizing IRS in the Central Highlands of Madagascar.	December 2013	January 2015	$280,000 (FY 2013)
Ongoing OR Studies FY 2015			
Title	**Start Date (est.)**	**End Date (est.)**	**Budget**
Evaluation of reactive case detection in the Central Highlands	September 2015	August 2017	$150,000 (FY 2014) + $313,000 (FY 2015)
Proposed OR Studies FY 2016			
Title	**Start Date (est.)**	**End Date (est.)**	**Budget**
Care-seeking behavior	December 2015	December 2016	$225,000

Plans and justification

PMI will also support an anthropological study to assess ITN use and barriers in different regions of Madagascar, in order to inform the NMCP on optimal ITN BCC messages and use with FY 2015 funds. With FY 2016 funds, PMI plans to support a study to inform the NMCP on reasons for delayed or non-care seeking behavior by caretakers of children and adults with fever, at the community and health facility levels. The NMCP requested PMI's support for a care-seeking behavior study as there are significant differences between regions in utilization of health care services that are not simply explained by access, but could be more linked to traditional practices, urban versus rural settings, or environmental factors. As indicated in the recent 2014 KAP survey, the majority of respondents knew what caused malaria and how to prevent it, yet awareness and knowledge of SP as prophylaxis and ACT as treatment were poor. Such a study would validate the hypothesis that differences in utilization are not explained by access alone, and enable the NMCP and partners to tailor messages to improve care-seeking behaviors.

Proposed activities with FY 2016 funding: ($235,000)

1. *Care seeking-behavior study:* PMI is proposing to support a study to inform the NMCP on reasons for delayed or non-care seeking behavior by caretakers of children and adults with fever, at the community and health facility levels. *($225,000)*

2. *Technical assistance to operational research activities.* Support for one CDC technical assistance visit to support operational research activities. *($10,000)*

9. Staffing and administration

Two health professionals serve as resident advisors to oversee PMI in Madagascar, one representing CDC and one representing USAID. In addition, two Foreign Service Nationals (FSNs) work as part of the PMI team. All PMI staff members are part of a single interagency team led by the USAID Mission Director or his/her designee in country. The PMI team shares responsibility for development and implementation of PMI strategies and work plans, coordination with national authorities, managing collaborating agencies and supervising day-to-day activities. Candidates for resident advisor positions (whether initial hires or replacements) will be evaluated and/or interviewed jointly by USAID and CDC, and both agencies will be involved in hiring decisions, with the final decision made by the individual agency.

The PMI professional staff work together to oversee all technical and administrative aspects of PMI, including finalizing details of the project design, implementing malaria prevention and treatment activities, monitoring and evaluation of outcomes and impact, reporting of results, and providing guidance to PMI partners.

The PMI lead in country is the USAID Mission Director. The day-to-day lead for PMI is delegated to the USAID Health Office Director and thus the two PMI resident advisors, one from USAID and one from CDC, report to the USAID Health Office Director for day-to-day leadership, and work together as a part of a single interagency team. The technical expertise housed in Atlanta and Washington guides PMI programmatic efforts.

The two PMI resident advisors are based within the USAID health office and are expected to spend approximately half their time sitting with and providing technical assistance to the national malaria control programs and partners.

Locally-hired staff to support PMI activities either in Ministries or in USAID will be approved by the USAID Mission Director. Because of the need to adhere to specific country policies and USAID accounting regulations, any transfer of PMI funds directly to Ministries or host governments will need to be approved by the USAID Mission Director and Controller, in addition to the US Global Malaria Coordinator.

Proposed activities with FY 2016 funding: ($ 1,645,000)

1. *In-country PMI staff salaries, benefits, travel, and other PMI administrative costs*: Continued support for two PMI (CDC and USAID) Resident Advisors and two Foreign Service National staff members to oversee activities supported by PMI in Madagascar. Additionally, these funds will support pooled USAID Madagascar Mission staff and mission-wide assistance from which PMI benefits. *($1,645,000)*

Table 1: Budget Breakdown by Mechanism

President's Malaria Initiative – MADAGASCAR

Planned Malaria Obligations for FY 2016

Mechanism	Geographic Area	Activity	Budget ($)	%
TBD – Supply Chain Contract	92 Districts	Procurement of ITNs for routine and continuous distribution	$6,120,000	30%
	93 Districts	Procurement of SP	$105,000	
		Procurement of parenteral artesunate for the treatment of severe malaria	$450,000	
	Nationwide	Procurement of laboratory consumables and reagents	$50,000	
	Nationwide	Warehousing and LMIS optimization	$400,000	
		Strengthen national capacity for supply chain management including implementing supply chain assessment recommendations	$800,000	
	92 Districts	Warehousing and distribution of ITNs	$1,700,000	
PSI	Sample of 92 Districts	ITN durability monitoring	$100,000	9%
	Nationwide	Support malaria BCC activities, including social marketing and malaria toolkit reproduction	$455,000	
CDC/IAA	Nationwide	Technical assistance to vector control activities	$14,000	2%

Project	Location	Activity	Amount	Percentage
		Procure entomological supplies	$12,000	
		Technical assistance to case management activities	$10,000	
		Technical assistance to support M&E activities	$10,000	
		Technical assistance to support OR study	$10,000	
		Staffing and administration	$380,000	26%
IRS 2 TO 6	East Coast and South East	IRS in 3 East Coast districts, and 1 South East district	$6,611,000	
	11 surveillance sites	IRS entomological monitoring	$225,000	
TBD	6 Regions	Support CHWs with MIP training and implementation	$150,000	9%
		Refresher training and supervision of community and facility-based case management	$1,600,000	
		Support for Malaria Peace Corps Volunteers	$12,000	
		Implementation of malaria BCC activities at community and health facility levels	$450,000	
MIKOLO Bilateral Project	9 Regions	Support CHWs with MIP training and implementation	$150,000	10%
		Refresher training and supervision of community and facility-based case management	$2,000,000	
		Support for Malaria Peace Corps Volunteers	$12,000	
		Implementation of malaria BCC activities at community and health facility levels	$500,000	

Partner	Location	Activity	Budget	Percentage
MCSP	Nationwide	Strengthen MIP at the facility level	$200,000	2%
	Nationwide	Conduct study on care seeking behavior	$225,000	
Malaria Care	Nationwide	Strengthening diagnostics and supporting national laboratory QA/QC program system including laboratory refurbishment	$400,000	2%
LMG	Nationwide	Strengthen the leadership, management, and governance for malaria leadership at the national level	$200,000	1%
Peace Corps	Nationwide	Support for Malaria Peace Corps Volunteers	$22,000	0%
TBD	Nationwide	Support Impact Evaluation	$100,000	0%
IPM	Nationwide	Support for Malaria Peace Corps Volunteers	$12,000	2%
		Continue support for 15 fever sentinel sites of the fever surveillance system	$300,000	
		Strengthen national disease surveillance system	$250,000	
MEASURE/EVAL	Nationwide	Strengthen HMIS and the NMCP's capacity to manage HMIS	$700,000	3%
USAID	Nationwide	Staffing and administration	$1,265,000	5%
Total			$26,000,000	**100%**

61

Table 2: Budget Breakdown by Activity
President's Malaria Initiative – MADAGASCAR
Planned Malaria Obligations for FY 2016

Proposed Activity	Mechanism	Budget Total $	Budget Commodity $	Geographic Area	Description
PREVENTIVE ACTIVITIES					
Insecticide-treated Nets					
Procurement of ITNs for routine and continuous distribution	TBD – Supply Chain Contract	$6,120,000	$6,120,000	92 Districts	Procure 1.85 million ITNs for routine distribution via EPI and ANC, and continuous distribution.
Warehousing and distribution of ITNs	PSI	$1,700,000	$0	92 Districts	Provide warehousing and distribution of routine and continuous distribution ITNs.
ITN durability monitoring	PSI	$100,000	$0	Sample of 92 Districts	Conduct year 1 of the ITN durability monitoring of ITNs distributed in Sept 2015. This activity builds on the previous ITN durability studies undertaken in Madagascar in 2013-2015.
Technical assistance to vector control activities	CDC/IAA	$14,000	$0	Nationwide	One CDC TDY to provide technical support for LLIN durability monitoring, and IRS related entomological monitoring.
Subtotal ITNs		$7,934,000	$6,120,000		
Indoor Residual Spraying					

62

Activity	Mechanism			Coverage	Description
IRS in 3 East Coast districts, and 1 South East district	IRS 2 TO 6	$6,611,000	$2,500,000	East Coast and South East	Conduct blanket IRS in 3 East Coast Districts, plus one expansion district in the South East.
IRS entomological monitoring	IRS 2 TO 6	$225,000	$0	11 surveillance sites	Conduct comprehensive IRS-related vector surveillance, assess resistance and other indicators of IRS impact: vector taxonomy and density, and insecticide decay rates. The 11 surveillance sites include current and former IRS areas.
Procure entomological supplies	CDC/IAA	$12,000	$12,000	Nationwide	Procure supplies for entomological monitoring.
Subtotal IRS		$6,848,000	$2,512,000		
Malaria in Pregnancy					
Support CHWs with MIP training and implementation	TBD	$150,000	$0	6 Regions	Provide training and implementation support for CHWs for MIP. Includes ITN use and referrals to health facilities for ANC and SP.
	MIKOLO Bilateral Project	$150,000	$0	9 Regions	
Procure SP	TBD – Supply Chain Contract	$105,000	$0	93 Districts	Procure ~500k treatments of SP. Funding includes distribution to districts.
Strengthen MIP at the facility level	MCSP	$200,000	$0	Nationwide	Support for MIP activities at the facility level, including strengthening and improving IPTp uptake, ITN use, and ANC attendance.
Subtotal Malaria in Pregnancy		$605,000	$0		
SUBTOTAL PREVENTIVE		$15,387,000	$8,632,000		

CASE MANAGEMENT

Diagnosis and Treatment

				Description
Procurement of parenteral artesunate for the treatment of severe malaria	TBD – Supply Chain Contract	$450,000	$450,000	Nationwide	Procurement of 113,400 artesunate vials and ancillary supplies, to complement the Global Fund commodities procurement. Funding includes distribution to districts.
Procurement of laboratory consumables and reagents	TBD – Supply Chain Contract	$50,000	$50,000	Nationwide	Procurement of laboratory supplies and reagents to support the revitalization of the national reference laboratory.
Refresher training and supervision of community and facility-based case management	MIKOLO Bilateral Project	$2,000,000	$0	9 Regions	Provide support to health facilities for management of CHWs. Activities will include refresher training, M&E integration, and routine supervision of CHWs. Activity will be co-funded by other USAID funding streams.
	TBD	$1,600,000	$0	6 Regions	
Strengthening diagnostics and supporting national lab QA/QC program system including laboratory refurbishment	Malaria Care	$400,000	$0	Nationwide	Provide support to build national capacity for QA/QC, including implementation of diagnostics assessment findings from 2014
Technical assistance to case management activities	CDC/IAA	$10,000	$0	Nationwide	One CDC TDY to provide technical support for case management.
Subtotal Diagnosis and Treatment		$4,510,000	$500,000		

Pharmaceutical Management

Warehousing and LMIS optimization	TBD – Supply Chain Contract	$400,000	$0	Nationwide	Support national supply chain management including warehousing and LMIS optimization for malaria commodities.
Strengthen national capacity for supply chain management including implementing supply chain assessment recommendations	TBD – Supply Chain Contract	$800,000	$0	Nationwide	Support national supply chain management by implementing supply chain assessment recommendations and quarterly end use verification at health facilities.
Subtotal Pharmaceutical Management		$1,200,000	$0		
SUBTOTAL CASE MANAGEMENT		$5,710,000	$0		

HEALTH SYSTEM STRENGTHENING / CAPACITY BUILDING

Strengthen the leadership, management and governance for malaria leadership at the national level	LMG	$200,000	$0	Nationwide	Support the USG efforts to strengthen the leadership, management and governance within the MoH. This activity is co-funded by other USG funding streams.
Support for Malaria Peace Corps Volunteers	Peace Corps	$22,000	$0	Nationwide	Support a third year malaria volunteer to coordinate malaria work with other PCVs in Madagascar. Funding breakdown is $12k to support the MV, plus $10k for SPA projects.
	IPM	$12,000	$0	Nationwide	Support a third year PCV to work on

Activity	Partner	Cost	Coverage	Description
	MIKOLO Bilateral Project	$12,000	9 Regions	implementation of malaria interventions. Funding will support PCVs nested with partners, and includes housing, transportation and equipment.
	TBD	$12,000	6 Regions	
SUBTOTAL HSS & CAPACITY BUILDING		$258,000	0	

BEHAVIOR CHANGE COMMUNICATION

Activity	Partner	Cost	Coverage	Description
Support malaria BCC activities, including social marketing and malaria toolkit reproduction	PSI	$455,000	Nationwide	Support the implementation of harmonized malaria messages at the community and health facility level. Funding includes revision of the malaria toolkit and reproduction of support materials.
Implementation of malaria BCC activities at community and health facility levels	MIKOLO Bilateral Project	$500,000	9 Regions	Support the implementation of harmonized malaria messages at the community level.
	TBD	$450,000	6 Regions	
SUBTOTAL BCC		$1,405,000		

MONITORING AND EVALUATION

66

Activity	Partner			Location	Description
Continue support for 15 fever sentinel sites of the fever surveillance system	IPM	$300,000	$0	Nationwide	Support 15 fever sentinel sites to monitor malaria throughout Madagascar. PMI will continue to work to integrate the management of the FSS into the national system.
Strengthen HMIS and the NMCP's capacity to manage HMIS	MEASURE/EVAL	$700,000	$0	Nationwide	Provide targeted support to the NMCP to strengthen the HMIS. Activities will include training, supportive supervision and materials.
Support Impact Evaluation	TBD	$100,000	$0	Nationwide	Provide operational support for Madagascar's Impact Evaluation
Strengthen national disease surveillance system	IPM	$250,000	$0	Nationwide	Targeted support to the NMCP for surveillance and epidemic detection.
Technical assistance to support M&E activities	CDC/IAA	$10,000	$0	Nationwide	One CDC TDY to provide technical support for M&E activities.
SUBTOTAL M&E		$1,360,000	0		
OPERATIONAL RESEARCH					
Conduct study on care-seeking behavior	MCSP	$225,000	$0	Nationwide	Support a study to inform the NMCP on reasons for delayed or non-care seeking behavior by caretakers of children and adults with fever, at the community and health facility levels.
Technical assistance to support OR study	CDC/IAA	$10,000	$0	Nationwide	One CDC TDY to provide technical support for operational research.

SUBTOTAL OR		$235,000		$0	
IN-COUNTRY STAFFING AND ADMINISTRATION					
Staffing and administration	USAID	$1,265,000	Nationwide	$0	Support for USAID annual staffing and administration, including CDC portion of ICASS.
	CDC	$380,000	Nationwide	$0	Support for CDC annual staffing costs.
SUBTOTAL IN-COUNTRY STAFFING		$1,645,000		$0	
GRAND TOTAL		$26,000,000		$17,264,000	

68